Keep Turning Left

by Ray Lambert

i

Dedicated to Darren and Sharon Boocock who were cut down just as they were getting started.

Also to all those riders who have lost their life in the pursuit of bringing entertainment to millions.

ISBN 978-0-9544519-5-0

Published by: RAYL, 13 Weedswood Road, Chatham, Kent ME5 0QR
Typeset by Richard Lloyd, Reading

FOREWORD

Keep turning left – three simple words that aptly describes what the world's fastest yet friendliest sport has involved over the last 85 years.

4-riders race 4-laps on a track with 4-turns measuring no more than 400 yards, BUT if only it was that easy!

This book capitalises on the level of competition that exists between Riders, their Managers and Promoters, and in some cases their ongoing battles with a plethora of rules and regulations which add further intrigue, suspicion and arguments.

Since the beginning of dirt track speedway at High Beech, via Wembley, to the present day setting of the magnificent Millennium Stadium in Cardiff, Riders, Officials and Fans have shown the world that despite the high level of competition and risk on the track and rivalry off it, there is no friendlier sport on the planet, nor I would suggest as many 'characters' in the sport.

It's no surprise really that Ray has managed to include so many stories into his book and I guess that he's had to leave out many, many more.

I know this book will evoke memories for supporters (past and present) and arouse a level of curiosity from others who have not yet had the privilege of being a speedway supporter.

Please enjoy.

Graham Reeve
Manager of the Speedway Control Bureau and the Great Britain Under-21 Team

By the same author:

Kent Ex-Boxers Association, 'Comes of Age', 1987

Nozzers, 2003

Nozzers First Class, 2004

Nozzers Go West, 2005

Nobbins, 2008

PREFACE

I first got the speedway bug just after the war in 1947 or maybe 1948, when things were beginning to pick up again. I was a very young man at the time but once I had seen my first meeting I was hooked. My enthusiasm knew no bounds and I happily rode my bicycle the ten miles from my home to The Firs Stadium, home of the Norwich Stars, most Saturday evenings.

Those were the days of Phil Clarke, Paddy Mills, Jack Freeman, Bob Leverenz, Billy Bales and, of course, the visiting teams would bring their top riders; men such as Jack Parker, Vic Duggan, Arthur Forrest, Tommy Price and a host of others. To me it was better than Hollywood film star parades. I even got to see my last of the leg trailers at The Firs, that was Bernie Slade riding for Bristol, although I believe that Bradford`s Oliver Hart continued to drag his leg for a year or so longer. Throughout the history of speedway, riders have always been prepared to meet, talk and sign autographs etc with the fans and that is what has given our sport the 'family image' that we have enjoyed over the years.

The stories in this book are stories that I have collected over several years and, to the best of my knowledge, they are factual and all good fun with nothing too controversial. The stories where people are quoted were given to me by the person concerned, well naturally or they wouldn`t be quotes. A lot of the earlier material, which was before my time, was told to me over a period of time by the master showman himself, Johnnie Hoskins. Johnnie was a mine of information and without his generous input this book would probably have only been about half the size – if it saw the light of day at all.

To acknowledge everyone that has contributed to (hopefully) make this book a success would take another book. I thank them all. They know who they are and we're still on friendly terms and that says it all, friendly people in a friendly sport.

This book is not a book of speedway facts and figures and only in one sense can it be viewed as speedway history. There are certainly a lot of interesting characters with interesting stories that have not made it to the following pages and I'm sure that certain readers will be disappointed that their favourite rider does not get a mention. No one said I was an expert or a statistician. I can only report what I know and I hope omissions, that are not deliberate on my part, plus of course (heaven forbid) any mistakes that have evaded my scrutiny, will not be judged too harshly.

This book is designed to be dipped into at any time without losing the place or the thread, it is arranged deliberately that way. I hope it has worked.

As you will see I have added a dedication at the beginning, which is my own personal indulgence and meant sincerely but I also dedicate it to the people who I hope will enjoy reading *Keep Turning Left* because without them I would have been enlightening myself.

Ray Lambert, 2010

Opinion

(All my own. No one else is to blame)

Current world champion Jason Crump has spoken out about the lack of protection afforded by Kevlars, the modern racing apparel. While the Kevlar material is adequate for most situations it offers little protection against friction burns as suffered by Crump and former world champ Nicki Pedersen and several other riders.

Having seen the evidence all it requires is for the powers-that-be to insist upon a return to genuine leathers for their riders' protection. It could mean sacrificing the loss of a few pounds of weight for the machine to carry but what is that when compared to horrific burns we have seen recently.

If riders are reluctant to discard the colourful Kevlars, they could always be worn over racing leathers.

After all it is not rocket science and one does not have to be a genius to put safety first.

~

A certain television commentator, whose name I can't bring to mind, always irritatingly predicts the result of every race before the riders have got past the first bend. *'If it stays like this it will be a 5–1, 4–2, 3–3',* or whatever. He educates us as the riders leave the gate. We know that and, in any case it rarely stays that way. In the main we all agree that they do a good job in keeping us informed but do we really need to know how clever they are. We are all capable of making up our own minds about what we're seeing in front of us.

The inter-heat summaries from messers Louis and Tatum on the other hand are most appreciated as are the analysis from the studio boffins; they add to the enjoyment and understanding but please Mr Commentator, very often one can't predict the outcome of a race even as the riders leave the last bend let alone entering the first.

~

Another gripe that needs looking into is (presumably) the television company's fault and their insistence upon showing us the 'gate stats'.

I believe I'm not alone in thinking that they are a complete waste of time and effort on someone's part in compiling what is useless information.

How often do we hear, *'Gate four is working particularly well,'* or *'There has not been a single winner from gate two all night.'* How often do we see the rider from gate four – or whatever gate it happens to be – get a clear blast around the others and have enough room to chop across the other three to take the lead. Conversely how often have we witnessed a rider getting left, or baulked and have to ease up only for him to let the others past and then power up the inside to take the lead. Or even a rider trying hard and looking for a gap for three and a half laps to suddenly find space on the last two bends and power through to the flag. Which begs the question – are these 'stats' still valid?

Even Johnnie Hoskins himself could never have visualised what he was starting when he introduced speedway racing to the public way back in 1923, in Australia.

For five years later, in 1928, he brought twenty riders and two promoters to England and the sport blossomed to such an extent that two years after they first set foot in England, there were seventy tracks operating throughout the country.

x

Johnnie Hoskins

Speedway supporters, riders, and anyone connected to the sport, have a lot to thank Johnnie Hoskins for, because Johnnie was the man who first saw speedway racing as a viable proposition and, hopefully, as a sport for future generations in his native Australia, and how right he was. A couple of years later he introduced the sport to England and from there, to the rest of the world.

He said, *'I well remember our very first race. I started off in front then, one by one, the other riders came hurtling past me. I vowed there and then that if I ever got out of there alive, it would be the other side of the fence for me.'*

Speedway

Johnnie brought his first riders over to England on the old ship *Oronsay*. The ship docked at Tilbury and off loaded twenty pioneer Australian riders with an assortment of bikes and bits of bikes. Little did any of them realise how quickly speedway would catch on.

Many years later, reminiscing about those days, Johnnie said: *'I like to think of the old ship Oronsay as the Mayflower of speedway'* and who could argue with that.

Speedway

Before he ever set foot on English soil Johnnies exploits had gone ahead of him and before he had left Australia he had an offer to manage ten tracks (mostly still to be built) around England.

Speedway

By 1935 Johnnie Hoskins had already acquired the title of *'The man that started it all'* – a tag that would stick with him throughout his long life. That year he took over management of West Ham speedway. The following year the West Ham Hammers finished bottom of the National League and Johnnie, ever the master showman, supplied the supporters club members with a miniature wooden spoon each, to hang on their club badges.

Speedway

After his early attempts and, as he says *'almost killing myself'* racing began to take a foothold in Australia and just prior to Christmas 1923 Johnnie managed

1

to get motorcycle racing on, albeit down the bill, at the Electric Light Carnival – named in honour of electricity just having been installed in the town.

Speedway

Johnnie, always a spinner of a good yarn, relates the tale from his West Ham days when skipper Tiger Stevenson was off form and just couldn't get to grips at all. He says, *'I had a mechanic called Alec Mosley and Alec gave Tiger's bike a good looking over but could see nothing wrong. Alec was a big lad and he got a large hammer and gave the bike an almighty wallop, telling Tiger that his frame had been all out of line. The psychology worked and Tiger went out and got a maximum that night!'*

Speedway

Canterbury speedway were obliged to get their complete programme finished by nine o'clock, due to the petty mindness of some local residents. This necessitated a strict seven o'clock starting time and hopefully no hold-ups and as Johnnie used to say, *'pray for no rain.'*

However, Johnnie had an ace up his sleeve as far as weather was concerned. RAF Manston was not far away and he would phone every race day to ascertain the current situation. He said: *'Those people were very good and always spot-on. Sometimes they would tell me to get finished as quickly as possible because the rain would come to the track a few minutes before nine – and it would come, right on cue.'*

Speedway

Johnnie always referred to his new enterprise as *speedway* although the Australian authorities insisted it was *motorcycle racing*. Even when he arrived in England the powers-that-be demanded *dirt bike racing* as a publicity title. Luckily he persevered and *speedway* soon became the sports official title, these days recognised throughout the world.

Speedway

'Canterbury was a nice place to officiate at especially when I shared the referee's box with Johnnie Hoskins, what a lovely man he was – and his wife was smashing too.' says Referee Barry Bowles.

Speedway

Fifty-six years after he first introduced speedway racing to the world, the 'Father of Speedway' Johnnie Hoskins was awarded the MBE – 'for services to motorcycling'.

On February 27, 1979 Johnnie arrived at Buckingham Palace to receive his honour from HRH Prince Charles. Asked by the Prince if he was a motorcyclist, Johnnie replied: *'I'm afraid not sir, I only promote the things!'*

Speedway

Johnnie tells a good tale about a home and away match between Coventry and Glasgow during the 1950s. Johnnie was promoter at Glasgow at the time and he recalled during the first leg, which was held at Glasgow, the Bee's top scorer had an engine failure on his way to the tapes. *'There was an unusual long delay while they worked on getting him started again and I was getting more and more agitated,'* he said. *'Then I realised that the grader was back out on the track. It was strange how it managed to stay out until that bike was working again.'*

For the second leg, this time at Coventry, he recalled that toward the end of the meeting the Bee's didn't have a single serviceable bike to wheel out. When suddenly there was a power failure and all the stadium lights went out. *'It was strange how by the time those lights were fixed they had two bikes out on the track ready to go,'* he said ruefully. *'Although I wasn't very happy that they managed to hoodwink us on both occasions, that was gamesmanship at its best.'*

Speedway

At West Ham's demise the developers built a housing estate on the site and named many of the streets after Hammers riders.

Johnnie had a nice little grassy banked, tree lined close named Hoskins Close, of which he was quietly proud.

Speedway

Johnnie started his working life as a telegraphist and at the outbreak of World War One, due to his knowledge of telegraphy, he was drafted into the Australian Navy as a Chief Petty Officer Telegraphist.

Manning a wireless station in Darwin, Johnnie is credited with discovering and plotting the position of the German ship Emden as it tried to get close to the Darwin coastline.

Speedway

Johnnie said: *'There are only two kinds of people in speedway – the ones that don't know the rules and break them and those who do know the rules and bend them.'*

The man that started it all, was star turn on ITV's 'This is your Life' in March 1974.

Four past world champions turned up to help him celebrate. They were Ove Fundin from Sweden, Ronnie Moore from New Zealand and Ivan Mauger and Barry Briggs, who were both in America at the time, flew over to be with Johnnie on his big night.

Speedway

The Canterbury speedway programme in August 1974 had this to say:

> *'Few promoters have served over twenty years as speedway managers without cracking up. One who hasn't any sense anyway has been at it for fifty years.'*

As Johnnie always wrote the programme notes himself, one can only speculate as to whom he was writing about.

Speedway

Johnnie Hoskins told the story of the rider who wouldn't have a bath after meetings: *'No matter where we were riding, this man would never go into the bathroom with the other riders after the meeting,'* he said. *'Some tracks in those days were a bit primitive but even the ones where we shared facilities with the football club, and they had a big bath tub or hot showers, this rider would still not go in, not even to wash his hands. He would load up his bike, change out of his leathers, and leave. He was not a particularly unfriendly character and when we got used to his phobia, or whatever it was, we just left him alone.'*

Pushed for the name of this unwashed rider, Johnnie would not budge. *'He was a good team member and we were glad to have him. It's an unusual story but the rest is his business.'* was all he would say.

Speedway

Over the years a lot has been written about Johnnie Hoskins, undoubtedly quite a lot of it generated by the master showman himself with some of that famous 'Hoskins spin' injected to add a bit of colour.

But 'The Man That Started It All' was generous enough to concede: *'If I hadn't started the ball rolling when I did, someone else would have done so soon after. Speedway was going to happen anyway!'*

4

Johnnie Hopkins Good wishes

Telephone
Herne Bay 5932

17 1·79

"Cliffside"
Manor Road
Bishopstone
Herne Bay

Dear Ray,
O.K. I will phone
you as I hear of the date.
of investiture.
I will be on the lookout
for Jan after the ceremony.
All the best
Yes
John mc.

Previous page : photograph by Ray Lambert.
Johnnie Hoskins shows MBE following his investiture
at Buckingham Palace, February 27, 1979.

Above : Letter from Johnnie to Ray referring to
arrangements to take photograph on investiture day.

6

Former SRA secretary George Barclay, in a philosophical mood but as usual, still talking a whole lot of sense. George, ever the diplomat, could make even an attack seem like a pleasant encounter.

'When I think of all the let downs I've encountered and the people I would like never to meet again, I wonder if I have wasted two years out of my life,' he says 'I refer, of course, to two years I spent securing funding for the Speedway Museum.

Whenever I get reminded of those folk, I just stop and think of the wonderful real Speedway fraternity I am privileged to be among.

Only two tracks refused us permission to hold a collection at their venue. All the rest not only gave us the nod, they went out of their way to make it a success. From Glasgow to Plymouth, all across the land we met magic supporters who gave not only their money, they gave us a welcome too. It was on such an occasion that I was reminded of those world champs trips to Poland again.

Sittingbourne boss Graham Arnold had invited us to collect at his track and as we passed the tuck shop there sat a man and his wife who kindly donated, when the lady said to me, "In my house I have a beautiful cut crystal vase, and every time I look at it I am reminded of you." She went on to explain that she had chosen this Polish glass item because of the quality for which it is famous. Sadly, she was at the back of the queue and the call was out for the coach to leave. Apparently, she reminded me, that I was able to apologise to the customers that we needed to jump the line, which they agreed to and the purchase was made. I feel humbled that not only does this lady remember, she feels it nice to remind and thank me.

A surprise? Not really. If you take away the not so genuine few, the overwhelming majority of the 'Speedway Family' are a wonderful fraternity to be part of.'

Rob Lyon, Great Britain team manager for the 2009 Speedway World Cup, concentrated on youth for the British team. Leaving the 'wags' to immediately christen the squad 'Young Lions'.

Exeter rider Ron Barrett had the unusual distinction of contesting a race on his own.

In 1952 at Southampton, three riders fell and were excluded from the re-run which left Ron a clear run home, more or less at his leisure. Then, within sight of three easy points his engine stopped, but there was just enough momentum left to allow him to free wheel to the chequered flag.

Although anger and frustration was nearing boiling point at a bad tempered meeting at Hackney in early August 1979, it couldn't be said that anyone involved saw red.

In what amounted to a double-header, with a Hackney v Eastbourne league match followed by the Vic Harding Memorial Trophy individual meeting, riders, team officials and spectators were all getting hot under the collar due to a combination of a delayed start, controversial refereeing decisions, and yet another long delay before the start of the second meeting, which eventually got under way after 10.30 pm – at a time when most meetings are over.

But the irritation reared up again when Hackney and Rye House second halfer Simon Aindow fell at the back of the heat quartet and although the track staff cleared his bike from the track – they left the rider where he was.

The remaining three riders, unaware of the fallen rider behind them, carried on and were confronted by Aindow still on the deck in the middle of the track when they arrived at the spot for the second time.

Luckily all three riders managed to avoid the fallen rider and only then did the red lights come on – as they entered the third lap!

Little Johnny Chamberlain filled in his time between race meetings for the Yarmouth Bloaters by waiting on tables at a nearby holiday camp.

Australian Jack Young was the first man ever to win the World Speedway Championship two years in succession. This he did in 1951 and 1952.

New Zealander Barry Briggs copied the same feat in 1957 and 1958, and Sweden's Ove Fundin followed suit in 1960 and 1961.

But another New Zealander, Ivan Mauger, eclipsed them all by taking a hat-trick of successive wins in 1968, 1969 and 1970.

While Dane Ole Olsen was celebrating his third World championship win at Wembley Stadium on Saturday September 2, 1978, English rider Gordon Kennett was reflecting on his runner-up placing and thinking of what could have been.

Gordon couldn't have picked a tougher year to make his first World Championship appearance. With ten of the sixteen riders winning at least one race apiece, it was one of the most competitive finals ever – and to top it all it was his birthday!

Being a last minute replacement for injured world champion Nicki Pedersen in the Latvian round of the 2009 Grand Prix, Peterborough's Danish rider Niels-Kristian Iversen was in a philosophical mood when being asked about how he thought the track conditions looked – bearing in mind that he was out in the first race. *'Pretty much the same as when I was here before,'* he said. *'We have to ride here anyway. It's still the same shape – and still the same way round!'*

Eastbourne, White City and all points north rider Steve Weatherley first sat on a grass bike in six inches of snow, in his back garden, during the winter of 1969. He first sat on a speedway bike the following year at the well known Iwade training school, under the tutelage of Barry Thomas.

Malcolm Craven started his speedway career in a hurry, he had a tryout at a training track in his home county of Essex – and broke the existing track record that had been established by the raceway founder in his very first race. Malcolm, a very useful team member for West Ham until his retirement in 1954, was also credited with playing the violin.

A speedway rider on the fiddle? Maybe he should have been a promoter.

As secretary to the Speedway Riders Association in late seventies George Barclay was invited to Wimbledon Stadium along with all the others in similar positions to dine and watch the meeting in the plush grandstand. The weather had been extremely wet and track conditions were far from good, but being a prestigious event *'it must go on'*.

In an early race the leading rider failed to turn at the end of the back straight and was stuck in the safety fence for the duration of the heat. More than put out by the heat not being stopped in the interest of safety, George went to the manager of the SCB and made the point to him. His reply? *'Well, no one goes there anyway'*.

Later in the same meeting George realised that the riders could not see in the wet conditions, so he went to the pits and asked the winning rider of the latest heat for his goggles, *'He was puzzled and if my memory still serves me it was John Louis. John agreed that I could borrow the glasses to show to the SCB manager. These goggles were opaque; there was no spot of vision anywhere through the lens. Those goggles were from the WINNING rider, not from one who had been filled in by the man in front. That manager staggered me with his question of why are you showing me these?*

I must add that the manager's wife was aghast at the condition of those glasses. She clearly realised the dangers the riders were exposed to.'

England's first World Champion Tommy Price suffered a fractured skull aged forty. Tommy said: 'After I had fractured my skull for the seventh time, my doctor advised me to give up speedway racing.'

Aussie Ron Johnson, riding for Belle Vue at New Cross in the summer of 1952, managed to wreck four bikes in four rides.

In his first outing it was his own, then in his following heats he borrowed (and wrecked) those of his teammates Denis Parker, Ken Sharples and Jack Parker.

$1$964 was not the best of years for Norwich shale superstar Ove Fundin because the four times world champion was obliged to face his nemesis Barry Briggs.

First, New Zealander Briggs raced to a unbeaten fifteen points maximum at Gothenburg Stadium in the world final to deprive Fundin, the reigning champion, of his crown. Then a short time after Briggs was at it again staking his claim for a title at the Golden Helmet, so long the property of Swede Fundin.

The first leg, raced at Oxford, was not a good start for holder Fundin who lost out 2-0 but that was not the end of the saga because at Norwich, Fundin's home track, where he hoped to turn the tables, he gated badly in their first race to watch Briggs romp home by thirty yards. In the second race Fundin showed the young pretender the way home after a grand first lap tussle only to blow his engine after the chequered flag, Even then, for the third race decider, it was not plain sailing because a bike borrowed from team mate Olle Nygren refused to function properly before the start and on a second mount, this time borrowed from Reg Trott, he led into the first bend only to watch Briggs power away down the back straight leaving him, on an unfamiliar bike, to lose the deciding race and the Golden Helmet that he had held for so long.

A name missing from the roll of world champions is that of Jack Parker, but Jack was the first ever world champion, he won the championship in 1931.

That first year the contest was run on a match race basis and Jack took the title by defeating Vic Huxley over three legs with the final leg being held at Wimbledon. The following year that championship was renamed the British Open Championship – so in fact 'the best rider never to be world champion' *was* actually world champion, and five years before anyone else!

For the start of the 1979 season Hackney teamster Sean Willmott's contract stipulated a 'no wedding for five years as a Hawks rider' clause.

The Danish leg of the 2009 Grand Prix, raced at Copenhagen had the vast crowds on the edge of their seats right up until the end with superb racing and passing throughout. To add to the excitement, both semi-finals were raced with only three riders.

In the first semi, new Russian sensation Emil Sayfutdinov, the meeting top scorer up until then, was excluded for touching the tapes, and then, in the second semi, world champion Nicki Pedersen pulled up with a puncture.

In his seven year career, to the close of the 1977 season Crayford's shale shifter Alan Sage had clocked up 265 consecutive appearances in official matches raced at West Ham, Ipswich and Crayford.

Canterbury rider Les Rumsey – or should that be Exeter rider Les Rumsey.... who can tell. Not even the man himself apparently.

With hardly enough time to get his leathers on Les was transferred from Canterbury to Exeter then loaned back by Exeter to Canterbury and then recalled to Exeter from Canterbury – it's fairly straight forward when you get the hang of it all, and even young Mr Rumsey must have got it straight in his mind eventually.

Reg Fearman, later promoter at several tracks, started his speedway career in 1948 by getting banned for being under age.

Later, whilst on loan to Stoke form his parent club West Ham in 1952, he crashed into the safety fence and came to a complete standstill during a race – but managed to keep his motor running.

Despite being left well behind, Reg got under way again and chased hard after the leading three eventually passing his own team mate and one of the opposition Liverpool riders. Then with an almighty swoop on the last bend of the last lap he dived under the race leader to take the chequered flag and the race win.

In a three week period in 1947, Yarmouth rider Billy Bales raced at seven different tracks, breaking the track record in six of the seven.

Crayford promoter Peter Thorogood had in mind the war years when he launched his 'school kids for 10p admission' to the Kestrels home meetings, during the school holidays of August 1976.

Peter said: 'We're not quite in the same situation as we were in the East End during the war but this inflation business is cutting deep and it's hard for families to keep ahead of rising prices. Here at Crayford we hope our gesture of greatly reduced childrens' prices for the school holidays will help with allowing families a night out at speedway.'

Wimbledon stalwart, Archie Windmill, who started his career way back in 1935 at High Beech, recalled breaking the track record at Hackney in 1939. He couldn't remember the new record that he created back then but says that it has never been bettered.

If Archie's memory served him correctly, then 1939 until Hackney's closure in 1996, is some long standing record!

Kent based, former Crusader, Les Rumsey, set off from home very early in the morning to attend the official practice day at his new club Exeter only to discover when he arrived that the Devon raceway was ankle deep in snow.

So Les turned round and headed back home only to learn, after travelling around 200 miles each way, that by the time he had reached home again that the County Ground snow had melted and practice went ahead (without him) as planned.

Raymond Humphreys, Stoke and Canterbury rider in the 1960s, changed his name to Tyburn Gallows, a name he adopted from his part time occupation as assistant public hangman. Humphreys used the *nom-de-plume* as a speedway rider but the Speedway Control Board objected and ordered him not to use the name. They also ordered that he remove a 'Ban-the-Bomb' sticker from his speedway bike.

Humphreys got around the Control Board demands by officially changing his name by deed poll and then there was nothing anyone could do or say, to the contrary. However, they had their own way regarding the 'Ban-the-Bomb' sticker.

Twenty-year-old Trevor Geer, an Eastbourne rider won a brand new JAP machine in a second half competition at his home track in 1973 and celebrate by scoring a maximum on it the following week.

Horses for Courses is a well bandied about saying within speedway. Boiled down it simply means that some riders negotiate certain tracks better than they do at others.

By way of illustration, a certain world-class rider and into the 'veteran' stage of his career, had dropped down a league to see out his twilight years, was asked how he found his new home track, *'You don't call this a bloody track do yer?'* he growled rather ungraciously.

Years later, during the 2009 Grand Prix series, a rider described conditions at one meeting as riding through chocolate.

While at a different meeting during the same series, another complained that it was *'like racing on concrete with marbles.'*

On the other hand, during the 2009 play-offs, a young second reserve told a TV interviewer, *'It's a really nice track out there.'*

12

Archie Windmill
Wimbledon, 1946

Danish star Hans Anderson, being philosophical during the 2009 Danish leg of the Grand Prix series held in front of his home country fans, said: 'Before I really enjoyed racing but running last and don't score the points, it's not that funny.' – where he had finished the night with only four points.

It never rains but it pours …. Peterborough Panthers lodged an appeal against Crayford for what they saw as use of an illegal silencer used by Kestrel's Mike Broadbanks in his first outing. The appeal was upheld and Broady's points were deducted and given to Peterborough. That then brought up another head scratcher, because it gave Peterborough three more points and they then used a tactical substitute later in the meeting which, with those three extra points (which they didn't know that manoeuvre was also illegal …. bring on the umbrellas.

Riding at Belle Vue, Arthur Atkinson suddenly found Eric Langton sprawling on the deck right in front of him.

Arthur recalled: 'It was impossible to miss him and I prepared to lay down my bike when I realised that Eric was directly between his bike and me. If I laid down I would have slid into him and he would certainly been injured, so I took the split second decision to run over him.

I shot up over his legs and machine and took off into space and straight for the wooden safety fence. I managed to bail out and in so doing winded myself. My bike was a wreck but Eric was OK.'

Arthur struggled through his final two races with a very painful ankle and a later X-ray showed his ankle to be broken. 'It took a month to heal.' he said ruefully.

Nigel Boocock always insisted in paying for the best helmets. Little Boy Blue who qualified for nine World Finals during his career in the top echelon of speedway said: 'I know it's a lot of money to pay for a helmet but helmets are very important.'

As if to emphasise that sentiment he came an almighty cropper whilst riding for Coventry at Leicester in October 1969 and his 'expensive' helmet was tested to the full and, in all probability, saved his life.

Nigel, Coventry's top rider, was matched against Leicester top man Ray Wilson when he came off heavily. The helmet split but absorbed most of the shock. Nigel was hospitalised with a fractured skull – but, as he said, 'What would have been the outcome without a good quality helmet.'

Wembley's high scoring former World Champion Tommy Price had a long and illustrious career but it was even longer than most people give him credit for because Tommy started on the two-wheeled road to fame as a seven year old, on an old motor bike that his dad bought for him that he would race around his back garden.

Jock Sweet – possibly one of the first riders to adopt the foot forward style that has become standard these days – as early as 1938, was asked, upon joining Norwich, if he had any superstitions. He replied that he had and that he didn't like to wear green or yellow. Imagine how he must have felt when he learned the Norwich colours were of all things green and yellow.

These days most top flight riders have their own mechanic to look after their equipment, particularly those with racing commitments in other countries, but not so long ago most riders only had the one bike in use and one track spare that could be used by anyone suffering problems – and usually one mechanic to look after the whole team. One such man was Cyril Spinks, chief mechanic of Wembley Lions in the 1950s. Cyril was asked to share his thoughts with a schoolboys' magazine. Here is his take on things:

'No rider can do his best without a well tuned bike but – make no mistake – the rider is more important than the machine in speedway. Bike of leading riders vary little. The engines are all virtually the same, 500cc JAPs developing about 45 brake horsepower. A typical machine today costs over £200. It has no brakes or gears and the only controls are those fitted on the handlebars, which control both throttle and clutch. A small tank carries a special fuel with which the bike does less than six miles to the gallon. The wheel base is much shorter than on the average road machine. One of the mechanics jobs is to make sure his teams bikes are correctly geared for the various tracks. Each one demands a different ratio.'

When Kings Lynn rider Chris Schramm isn't shifting shale he is to be found at the family's 'Pet Crematorium' in Essex. With his insider knowledge he should be a wow at the annual Speedway Burn-up Bonanza each November.

One wonders if they have a doctor on duty at trackside at the Broken Hill raceway in New South Wales, Australia, or whether they call upon the Flying Doctor, who have one of their South East Section's nine Divisions based there.

Johnnie Hoskins recalled two top class heat partners he had in a team that he was promoting. 'They were almost like Siamese Twins,' Johnnie said. 'It felt at times watching them that you could have tied their respective inside elbows together, they were that close. You could have been forgiven for thinking that they were telepathic the way they worked together side by side on the track .... the problem was, off the track they never spoke to each other!'

Unfortunately Johnnie would never divulge the names of these two strange characters.

In 1950, on a memorable night in Norwich, Tommy Price was pitted against the Stars top scorer Paddy Mills in Match Races.

Tommy said: 'I won both races but it tough going up there against Paddy, particularly as I had never been on the old Firs track before.'

Brian Havelock, these days team manager for the Redcar Bears in the Premier League, recalls an incident from his time whilst riding for the Newcastle Diamonds. The Diamonds had been riding away at Glasgow and after the meeting he was driving back south down the M74 in his car following fellow Diamonds Tom and Joe Owen in their car.

He says: 'After about two hours Tom Owen pulled off the motorway to stop for a cup of tea. This involved going over the motorway to the services, which were on the Northbound side. After a stop of about half an hour Joe decided to drive their car the rest of the way home. I set off, over the bridge and onto the Southbound carriageway but, for some reason Joe didn't follow me and he took the nearest lane which, naturally was Northbound. Tom had fallen asleep almost immediately and Joe drove all the way back to Glasgow before he realised what he had done.' 'There were no mobiles in those days and I found out later that the air was all shades of blue for some time after that and Joe was not allowed to drive the car for quite a while.'

Canterbury stalwart Graham Banks died as the result of an on-track accident at a grass event on June 4, 1978 and, after the funeral service, the Crusaders did their own special accolade to his memory that same night at Kingsmead Stadium.

Before their league match against Milton Keynes Graham's racing equipment and floral tributes were given a lap of honour on the back of his old pick-up that he was so fond of.

Reg Trott
in Wimbledon colours

Best wishes
Reg Trott

A decade or so later Mildenhall rider Mick Bates went down the same route as Reg Trott, the same route that all potential referees have to take but Mick didn't recall the opposition to the changeover that Reg had endured.

'I don't recall having a hard time at all,' he said. *'maybe Reg smoothed the way for me and my transition was that much easier than his.'*

Mick also made the grade as a referee and, like Reg, has enjoyed many seasons in the *hot seat*. To date Reg Trott and Mick Bates are the only two riders to have qualified as speedway referees.

The old concrete starting gates last saw the light of day in 1956. An SGB ruling stated that 'all concrete starting gates must be covered over by July 1, 1956.'

The heavens opened up at Sheffield a few years ago and the rain came down in torrents badly affecting the track. Then suddenly singing started up and soon the whole crowd were in unison as they joined in singing in the rain.

Barry Bowles was the referee and he recalls: *'Believe it or not the rain stopped. But my question was, is this a plea to the Almighty to turn the taps off, or was it in response to the dreadful noise that he could hear coming up from the Owlerton choir.'*

Edinburgh rider Aaron Summers contested his first ever Elite League race at Wolverhampton, as a guest for Lakeside, in the prestigious play-offs of 2009, only to have the ignominy of breaking the tapes and having to start off a fifteen-metre handicap, which saw him trail home in last place. He followed that up with three more last places – not the most auspicious of top-flight debuts. It wasn't all bad luck however because he was able to get a 'first class view' of the races from his vantage point behind the other three riders.

Coventry's Nigel Boocock (little boy blue) and Swindon's Mike Broadbanks (the red devil) are usually regarded as the first two riders to buck the trend by wearing coloured leathers, with their blue and red racing suits respectively. However, something like ten years earlier, Glasgow's Ken le Breton (the white ghost) and West Ham's Malcolm Craven (little boy blue) beat Booey and Broady by a decade. A further decade later, black leathers were the odd ones out and a decade after that almost every rider had their own personalised leathers in almost every colour one could think of.

Before the days of mobile phones and in-car satnav systems, Ray Bales found himself with a puncture and everywhere closed down for the night. He said: 'I was travelling home from the old Reading track after a nights racing when I got a puncture in the trailer wheel although I didn't realise it until the tyre came right off the rim. With no spare, I found a telephone box and called Trevor Hedge. I knew Trevor would still be up at that time of night. Trevor told me to call back and when I did about ten minutes later, he said that Jim Tebby had a mini wheel that I could use.

Jim's mini was about fifteen miles away, so I unhitched the trailer and left it on the roadside just outside Reading and went looking for the address that Trevor had given me. I found the mini but I didn't have a car jack but managed to lift the car up on bricks to get the wheel off.

Suddenly there was flashing blue lights as the 'neighbourhood watch' had called the police. A bit of fast-talking didn't convince them and they said I should put the wheel back. A bit of radio talk followed and finally they got someone at the police station to contact Jim Tebby who confirmed that it was OK to have the wheel.

All's well that ended well and that policeman warned me that if this should happen again it should be within normal working hours. I don't think he knew that for a speedway rider this was normal working hours.'

Long time Silver Helmet holder Tom Owen, said that he hardly ever did any practice despite carving out a makeshift track on his farm. He said: 'I rarely did any practice, either on my own or at official practice days, home or away, I just used to arrive at the starting gate, drop the clutch and go.'

In his first season 1974, sixteen year old Steve Weatherley contested the Junior Championship of the British Isles and scored five points. The following year he was at it again, this time just running second to new champion Neil Middleditch in a run-off. The next year he was just unlucky once more when, in a close fought contest with eventual winner Michael Lee, he again was placed second.

Swede Peter Karlson was in a philosophical mood during the Elite League play-offs. The Wolverhampton captain said: 'I've had gremlins everywhere I go, they seem to follow me.' – then he tried his second bike, and got knocked off!

John McGuinness, high flying tarmac racer and the fastest man around the Isle of Man TT circuit, paid tribute to his opposite numbers on the shale: *'These guys make it look easy from the terraces but it's not,'* he said. *'I like to watch speedway whenever I can, and when I'm racing if there's a track operating nearby on the same night I go and watch. I bought a bike from Jason Crump so I could have a go myself but it spends most of its time in the garage.'*

John said that when he's racing on the road circuits he gets the other riders to watch speedway on the television in between races in his sponsors hospitality room.

Nigel Boocock became 'half Australian' as, he says, when he moved 'down under'.

Little Boy Blue was granted a New South Wales license when he moved with his family to Sydney – but still raced for Canterbury in the UK the following season.

For the 2010 season the Royal Navy will continue its relationship with the Elite League Lakeside Hammers and the logo is proudly worn on team race suits and around the Arena Essex Stadium.

Cdr Steve Pearson RN said, *'The link up has been really successful after the Sky meetings last season and we saw increased interest in the Royal Navy through our website and also interest from people who had seen us as part of the television broadcast. The report of the link up in Speedway Star has again helped promote the Royal Navy across the sport and we are delighted to be involved again.'*

Philip Morris spent most of his racing career with Reading but spent the last four years flitting around Newcastle, Belle Vue, Newport, Lakeside and Stoke. He recalled: *'I had a bit of a run in with Peter Carr once at Edinburgh and many fans used to boo me after that; basically, they weren't very fond of me up there. Then, out of the blue, John Campbell the promoter rang me and asked if I would guest for the Monarchs at Berwick. Even as a guest the fans were still not pleased to see me and I didn't help matters by turning in three average rides in my first three outings but I managed to win them round with victories in heats 13 and 15 which won the meeting. That changed the atmosphere and I received a standing ovation from the travelling Edinburgh fans.'*

igel Boocock, in Canterbury colours

End-of-season flour fight

One of England's best known referees, Tony Steele, has been around speedway since 1969 but it was not until 1994 that he took up refereeing duties. Since then he has officiated at tracks all around the country and abroad including Ice Racing on the continent. He says: '*I remember one of my early jobs was not so auspicious. As a trainee in 1994 I had the task of chasing rabbits off the track at Ipswich.*'

Like Winston Churchill before him, Trevor Geer had his *finest hour*. He recalls: '*It was the first time I ever rode for Wembley. I was No. 8 for the Lions and was on cloud nine out there on parade in a stadium with so much history. Trevor Redmond was announcing the teams and when he came to me on the end of the line, he came up with those immortal words, "and riding at No. 8 tonight we have .... er .... What's your name lad?" That certainly burst my bubble!*'

Aussie Bert Spencer started his riding career at Brisbane in 1927 and arrived in England the following year where International Speedways Ltd snapped him up. He managed to ride for Wimbledon, Harringay, Stamford Bridge and White City Manchester during that first year in this country. The following year he settled with Exeter and the year after with Leicester before captaining Plymouth from 1931 until the end of the 1933 season.

For 1934 and 1935 Bert broadened his horizons by taking on America, mostly in San Francisco and Los Angeles. 1936 he was back with Wimbledon and a spell at Bristol before returning to Wimbledon and being loaned out to Norwich where he became a full time Norwich team member in 1937.

In the eight years since he first started (excluding the two years spent in the USA and including three spells at Wimbledon) Bert Spencer rode for eleven different teams before ending up at Norwich.

Wimbledon rider Ron How recalled one of his many trips to Poland, where he was not left in the dark. He said: '*We were in the middle of a meeting when the stadium lights went out. It was too dark to race without lighting so they drove their cars around the outside of the track and turned their headlights on so the meeting could continue. It wasn't too successful though because there was dark patches and some bits too bright and some places with headlights right in your eyes. The Poles didn't appear to mind though, they were crazy riders in those days.*'

Ron Howe

Transfer Fees

S peedway's first £1,000 transfer fee changed hands as early as 1935. That's what Wembley paid Belle Vue for Frank Charles.

Speedway

In 1952 a speedway record transfer fee was paid to Edinburgh for reigning world champion Jack Young. West Ham paid the modest fee (by today's standards) of £3,750 for Aussie Jack and that figure remained a record for more than twenty years.

Speedway

Motherwell's transfer listed Stan Bradbury was offered as a £250 'bargain' but Stan himself complained to the Control Board that the price was too high. The Board obliged by reducing it to £75!

Speedway

When New Cross closed down in 1953 the three Roger brothers had to find new bases from which to ply their craft. Cyril Roger went to Norwich for £1600, Bert Roger went to West Ham for £1600, but younger brother Bob Roger only rated £200 on his transfer to Birmingham.

Speedway

For his second year of racing, Eastbourne transferred Pete Jarman to Stoke. *'They really wanted me badly up at Stoke,'* Pete cracked, *'because they paid the massive transfer fee of twenty-five quid!'*

Speedway

When Eastbourne's Gordon Kennett was transferred to Oxford for £1,500, younger brother Barney wanted to top his brother's fee. So his, for his transfer from Canterbury to Hackney, he asked for a higher price. Hackney obliged with £1,500.01 – one penny more!

Speedway

When West Ham paid the then record transfer fee for reigning world champ, Jack Young in 1952, they expected great things from him. Young duly obliged by winning the world title for his new team again that same year.

'Aussie' Jack contested three more world finals after his record setting two-wins-on-the-trot triumph, 1953, 1954 'and 1955, racking up 10, 11 and 10 points respectively.

Speedway

Charlie Knott, promoter at Southampton, wanted Jack Parker to join the Saints as team captain. When they met Charlie got out a roll of pound notes and asked Jack how much it was going to take to get Jack into his team.

Jack replied: *'You keep counting over the money and I'll tell you when to stop.'* Charlie was glad when Jack called stop at £500.

Speedway

Well travelled shale shifter Pete Jarman is proud of his record transfer fee. In 1964 Pete was transferred from Stoke to Wolverhampton for a record fee of £500. That was in the days of the old Provincial League and the following year leagues were amalgamated to become the British League, so the Provincial League was no more. *'That means the record is mine whatever happens.'* Pete declared.

Speedway

In February 1952 Australian International rider Aub Lawson was allocated to Norwich for a fee of £1,500, only a month after the Control Board had sanctioned his move to West Ham. Lawson's berth with the Hammers was conditional upon Jack Young not returning to England from his native Australia but, even as the papers were being signed, Young was reported to be already on his way. That meant that Lawson was reassigned to either Wimbledon or Norwich, and Norwich needed his services because yet another Australian, Bob Leverenz, was unable to return to the Stars ranks because of ill health.

When Bruce Penhall won the world championship at Wembley Stadium on September 5, 1981, he was the first American to win the title since Jack Milne achieved the feat in 1937. The young Cradley Heath rider did one better than his fellow countryman though because the following year, on August 28, he repeated the feat on his home turf Los Angeles, at the Memorial Coliseum.

Penhall achieved both his world titles with fourteen points (from a maximum of fifteen), and by coincidence, he dropped his only point at Wembley in his first race, and in Los Angeles he dropped his only point of the meeting in his last heat.

Speedway rules state that riders must wear gloves and Edinburgh Monarchs home team rider Tommy Miller learned to his cost that rules must be obeyed.

In a Britain v Overseas international meeting at Edinburgh in August 1952, Miller, who had been working on his engine until the very last minute before his race, rushed to the starting gate with his gloves still stuffed into his body colour – and was promptly excluded for holding up the start while he put his gloves on.

During the filming of The Sweeney in 1976, there was one segment filmed at London's White City and Trevor Geer was taken on to play the part of the villain's friend.

'The scene was,' Trevor recalled, 'that I would do a couple of laps with my White City team mate Paul Gachet, and as I came back to the pits, John Thaw, who was the policeman, would arrest me. But before I went out on the track the film crew told me to move out into the dirt on the outside where John Thaw was leaning on the fence. This I did and John was lost in a cloud of dust. When I got back to the pits John was busy dusting himself down and the air was rather blue. I explained that I did what I was told to do and that it was the crew's idea. I think he saw the joke.

We had a really good day filming with him, he was a super guy and a great shame when he died later whilst filming Morse.'

A bit of speedway history was made on July 17, 1978, at Exeter. This took the form of a double header, not that double headers are history-making epochs in themselves normally. But on this particular occasion Exeter Falcons met Hackney Hawks in a league match and then faced the same opponents again in a KO Cup match. The Falcons ran out comfortable winners both times, putting the Hawks to flight 56–22 and 58–20.

All's well that ends well and Oxford rider Trevor Geer was glad there was some truth in that old saying when he dived up the inside of Soren Sjosten and left him sprawling on the deck. He says: *'I was feeling pretty pleased with myself as I went back to the pits until I was told by the rest of the team that Soren was not one to take such incidents kindly and that he would probably want to kill me when the doctor had finished with him. We did have a few words, and we ended up good friends when I agreed to wait for him to have a couple of beers after the meeting and then drive him to Heathrow for his flight back to Sweden.'*

Brian Shepherd has cause to remember the August Bank Holidays of 1951 and 1952. The Cradley Heath rider crashed on that date in 1951 and suffered a broken leg which kept his out of the saddle for a full year. He made his comeback on the same date a year later and scored his first ever maximum.

International speedway star John Davis had the unusual experience of being booked as a guest rider – to replace himself!

For the start of the 1975 season Davis was contracted to ride for Oxford but just prior to Oxford's opening night, he was re-allocated to Reading. However, on the very day the contracts became final he was booked to ride for Oxford as a guest rider in a meeting against Coventry – to fill a gap in Oxford's ranks left vacant by his move to Reading.

One can only speculate upon what the outcome would have been if the opposition on that night had been Reading instead of Coventry.

Yarmouth's pint-sized rider, Johnny Chamberlain, did a lot of travelling for his first meeting in this country. 'Aussie' Johnny, newly arrived from Australia, was pressed straight into service by the East Anglian club – and his first race was in Scotland.

George Newton, not blessed with the best of health, was so exhausted after a particularly tough race early in 1949, that he collapsed after passing the chequered flag and fell off his bike and bashed his nose.

Peterborough's Danish international star, Niels-Kristian Iversen, finally to got ride in a Grand Prix final and, as luck would have it, in front of his home country fans in Copenhagen. As a wild card entry for the 2009 Danish round on June 14, Iversen made it through to the final with eleven points but finished in last place. An elated but at the same time sad Niels said: *'My first GP final and in front of my home fans – I'm a bit disappointed to come last.'*

29

Just prior to a league match at West Ham on July 22, 1952, Wimbledon rider Ernie Roccio, who had experienced car trouble on his way to the venue, joked: 'This will not be my lucky night.'

Those words proved to be very prophetic and certainly no joke because 'American' Ernie crashed into the safety fence during the very last heat of the meeting and died three hours later from his injuries.

Speedway's tough guy George Newton retired in 1938, and made a come-back ten years later in 1948. George, then a New Cross rider, suffered a serious illness in the July of his comeback year, which meant the removal of a lung, but even that couldn't stop the human whirlwind.

Later, in 1950, George was sidelined with a broken leg as a result of a crash in France but even that couldn't keep him out of the saddle – he was back riding inside of a month, with his leg still in plaster. He finally retired in 1953 having also slid his way around Walthamstow, Fleetwood, Harringay and St. Austell tracks, among others.

Olle Nygren was always a well travelled man and particularly so in the mid 1950s.

His longest trip was 1954-55 driving down to South Africa from Stockholm and back via the Congo and Nigeria route, a distance (the way Olle went) of almost five thousand miles.

Of course, regular commuters to Downunderland will have clocked up far more miles but Olle did his the old fashioned way, with his feet, or at least his wheels, firmly on the ground.

Olle competed in speedway meetings in South Africa again the following year, 1955-56, for a couple of months, and a year later, 1956-57, he was out there again riding for Trevor Redmond. That winter he also took his AJS 7R and took part in several tarmac meetings against such notables as Mike Hailwood, Gary Hocking and Jim Redmond. In between times he took a Scandinavian team out there for a three months spell.

Then, in 1971-72, Olle took a Swedish team on a four-month tour of Australia and New Zealand, where he says he organised everything himself.

Not surprisingly Olle is a Member of the Swedish Sports Academy.

Ernie Roccio
Died of his injuries July 23, 1952

A victory parade after a home match in May 1963 spelt disaster for Sheffield rider Guy Allott. He fell off the tractor and was trapped under the heavy metal grader. When rescuers managed to free him, they found that Guy had a punctured lung and a broken arm, plus injuries to his face.

What a way to celebrate a victory!

The Reading team used to travel on northern tours in a Chalfont 55 seater coach, with the back 16 seats taken out to accommodate the bikes. Some of the riders felt a bit bashful at first with the strange looks they received at their destination, with team management, riders and mechanics all piling out of the same coach.

John Louis thanked his lucky stars that he had a very reliable bike for the 1972 World Final at Wembley because while he was otherwise engaged out on the shale, someone got into the pits and stole his second mount.

John said: ' I went out in my race and all the gang went to watch me race; never giving a thought to security, after all it was a secure area. Meanwhile someone managed to get into the pits and wheel my spare bike out, right past two rather large security guards on the gate.

When I came back in, somebody asked where the spare had gone and, of course, no one knew. We searched everywhere all to no avail and I had given up ever seeing it again. After the meeting we eventually found that bike hidden behind a hot dog stand. Luckily my first choice bike was reliable enough to see me through.'

Louis finished the night in fifth place with eleven points. The next time the World Final was held at Wembley, three years later, He powered to a rostrum place with a third place.

Nigel Boocock was riding at Wolverhampton and his team mate Barry Briggs drove up from his Southampton home to Nigel's home in Rugby. Barry's wife stayed with Nigel's wife at home while the two riders travelled up to Wolverhampton in Briggo's car with the bikes on his trailer.

Almost as soon as the meeting started Briggo came a cropper and was taken to hospital. From the hospital he phoned the wives to let them know, and while he was on the phone he said, 'Oh, just hang on a minute, they've just brought Booey in!' Nigel had managed to come a cropper as well.

Plodding on

Mildenhall rider Mick Bates was never one to let the grass grow under his feet on the track and since his retirement from the shale shifting business he's not been idle either.

Mick is only the second rider ever to be accepted as a speedway referee after his riding days were over, and later he joined the Norfolk Constabulary, where he travelled around the county with various divisions and in various jobs, including CID and the Drugs Squad, until he says, *'After twenty seven years, these days I get to sit behind a desk as an Inspector.'*

Speedway

John Hibben's bike was a lot more powerful than most of his fellow team members because John's everyday job was as a motorcycle cop with the Metropolitan Police.

John, a regular team member with Canterbury for the 1968-69, also rode for Romford, which was right on his doorstep. He recalled: *'I was getting a few second-half rides around Romford when team member Ian Gills broke his leg and they asked me to fill the vacant spot until Gills was fit again.'*

When Gills returned to the team, John thought he was out of a job but the club gave him second-halves for the remainder of the season, as a thank-you for helping them out.

Although John Hibben tended to approach speedway as more of a hobby – due to his off-track occupation with the police force – he was nevertheless a force to be reckoned with, as many riders and promoters of the era will testify.

Speedway

Jim Lawrence started his career with the Metropolitan Police and graduated to motorcycles in 1987, where he stayed until 1990 before moving on to beats new.

In 1995 he was undergoing referee training at Ipswich, under the guidance of Lew Stripp when, he says, Lew gave an unpopular decision against one of the Ipswich riders to the annoyance of the Witches promoter. The promoter made his feelings very clear by shouting: *'That's the worst decision I have ever heard of – and a thousand fans agree with me.'*

To which Lew replied: *'If you were doing your job properly it would have been ten thousand!'*

Like all good trainees Jim learned from Lew's handling of that situation because a few years later and fully qualified in his own right, he was able to put his early teaching to good use.

In a Monday night league match in 2008, at Bell Vue where Swindon were the visitors, Jim excluded a Swindon rider for some infringement and team manager Alun Rossiter was not best pleased. *'That's the worst decision I have ever seen,'* he ranted in true Rossiter style. *'Well give it time,'* Jim replied, *'after all it's only heat four!'*

Former Mildenhall whiz-kid Mick Bates, who later moved to the other side of the fence and is still currently officiating as a referee around the east coast, joined the police force in 1983 in his home county of Norfolk. While doing his early training in Norwich he was soon rubbing shoulders with the celebrities of the day. Mick remembered those early tentative steps as one of the boys-in-blue, *'One of my very first jobs as a young probationer was to babysit Frankie Goes to Hollywood in an hotel right in the centre of Norwich.'* he said. *'Then, soon after that I got my maiden arrest. I had to make an arrest for a traffic violation – and the car driver turned out to be Adam Faith's brother.'*

Just like so many people in speedway, referee Barry Bowles had a mischievous streak in him, and one day at Peterborough promoter David Hawkins was working himself up into a right state due to a shortage of riders, as a result of injuries etc. and was toying with the idea of borrowing a junior from the visiting team – if they had a spare. So Barry decided to add to promoter Hawkins' agitated state with a joke of his own: *'On my way from the pits to the referees box I stopped and addressed the crowd on the first bend,'* he said. *'"Can anyone here ride a motorbike?" I asked, and some people showed interest so I continued, "If you go to the pits you may be able to help out." I believe several did too. Mr Hawkins and I had a great relationship right up until he left the club but he was not around that night when I took my paperwork to his office after the meeting – I wonder why?'*

Terry Barclay retired from the shale after receiving a badly cut heel in a fall at Canterbury but he didn't move far from the two wheeled business. Soon after he applied and was accepted into the police force and, after initial training in Sussex, moved into the traffic division where he began his instruction on motorcycles.

Being an experienced speedway rider Terry needed very little teaching on motorbikes and he delighted in upsetting the instructor by staying close behind him every time he tried to race away before turning around to see how far behind he had left *the learners*.

As with most young speedway riders, Terry was old enough to ride a speedway bike but not legal to ride a bike on the road, or drive a car for that matter, during his time on the shale. However, as time went on, he qualified to drive police cars in addition to motorcycles. Later he became the 'collector' of firearms when the law demanded they be handed in.

Speedway

Probably the first policeman to be accepted as a speedway referee was Detective Constable Barry Richardson of the Somerset Police Force. Barry recalled the day when he was able to combine both jobs at the same time. He said: *'I was the-man-on-the-button at Swindon in the early 1980s. It was very bad weather and in heat one a rider from the visiting team got filled in completely. After the first lap he stopped and put his bike across the track, in front of the starting gate, as a protest. I asked him to remove it but he refused, so I fined him. With that he stormed up to the referee's box to remonstrate. All I could see was two white rings around his eyes where he taken off his goggles. He shouted at me: "I'll hit you and you can call the police if you like." I replied: 'I am the police!" A few days later, after he'd had time to calm down, he did send me a nice letter of apology.'*

Speedway

While patrolling his Leicester City beat in 1991, Jim Lawrence noticed Billy Hamil's well sign-written van heading through the city, presumably heading for a speedway meeting somewhere which Jim guessed would be Kings Lynn. Later that night Jim and his colleagues saw Billy in his van going in the opposite direction, probably heading for the M1 and home. This was years before Jim became a referee. Jim said: *'We flagged him down because he was speeding a little through the City but mainly I just wanted a chat to learn how he had got on. We approached the van at the nearside window; there were two or three others inside. One of my colleagues asked for the driver's name and Billy must have thought that he was in trouble because he gave a false name. I said, that's funny. The last time I saw you your name was Billy Hamil!'*

35

City of London policeman Barry Bowles was on his way to referee a meeting at Eastbourne in May 1984. Barry always liked to leave home very early when officiating at Eastbourne so that, with his family in his car, they could spend some time in Eastbourne or at Beachy Head prior to the meeting.

On the way he pulled into a lay-by near Hailsham so they could all enjoy a cup of tea and a sarnie before arriving at Arlington Stadium, when he was smashed into from behind. His car was wrecked but Barry and the family appeared OK at first and he was able to check on the other driver, an elderly lady who tried to drive away but her front wheel fell off.

As luck would have it, an off duty ambulance man stopped on his way to work, and then an off duty policeman also stopped, which meant they were all looked after before taken to hospital with head injuries and whiplash. Naturally Barry had to contact Eastbourne Stadium to inform them that he would not be arriving to officiate. He was off work for eighteen months and even after that only on light duties.

Three years later Barry was retired from the police force on health grounds as a direct result of his injuries. The other driver was charged with Careless Driving, a charge that was reduced from Dangerous Driving because Barry was a police officer, even though she had actually gone over a grassy bank before ploughing into his car at forty miles an hour. Then in 1992 it was discovered that Barry had broken his neck in the accident.

He said: *'That crash cost me more than my career with the police it cost me my elevated status, because, before the accident I was six feet two inches, and nowadays I've been reduced to five eleven!'*

Later Barry became secretary of the Referees Association and retired from the position in 1995.

Down in the countryside in the south of Norfolk, where inspector Mick Bates is currently strutting his stuff, there is a large workforce of Eastern Europeans and Mick and his crew had to arrest a couple of them for burglary at a nearby farm. *'Initially they said they couldn't speak English,'* said Mick *'but when I told them I had been to Latvia a few times, and particularly at Daugaupils where I had officiated at the speedway stadium, that broke the ice!'*

Vaclav Verner, Czechoslovakian star at Exeter was a Prague policeman for ten years in the 1970s. Like most Czechs at the time, he rode for the police owned Red Star team at the Marketa Stadium. Although, as he says, he graduated all the courses and training, he was discharged from the police in 1980 *'for scandalous talk against the communist regime.'*

Barry Bowles tells the story about the only time that he ever changed a refereeing decision throughout his whole refereeing career:

'There had been a coming together and two riders fell and I excluded one of them as the primary cause of the stoppage. There was a big reaction from the crowd and then, the sound of a steel shoe on the stairs leading to the referee's box. A breathless rider that had been involved in the stoppage came in and said "You're wrong ref." As he was being polite, I asked him why and he replied with great credit to him and to my amazement "Because it wasn't him. It was my fault. I caused it." .... he then went on to describe what had happened in great detail. There were great cheers from the crowd when the reversal of my decision was announced and especially for that rider's honesty. I just wish that I could remember that man's name.'

One Saturday lunchtime in 2007 speedway referee Jim Lawrence was at his day job with the Leicestershire police, sitting in the canteen with several of his colleagues and the talk was about speedway. Jim said:

'By coincidence a few minutes later a call came in from a marked patrol car that was sitting outside a petrol station saying that someone had pulled out of the petrol station and instead of turning left to join the traffic flow he'd turned right, straight across the oncoming traffic and across the central reservation to join the traffic flow going in the opposite direction on the other side of the dual carriageway.

When they pulled the car over they found the driver was Billy Janerio, and Billy explained that, to save time, he had cut across. He was very apologetic but said that he was pressed for time to get to a speedway meeting and hadn't seen the police car.

They told him that one of the bods at the station was a speedway referee and they asked me if I could do anything to help the situation. As they hadn't written him up and as Billy had been cooperative and polite we agreed to let him off with a rollicking and flag the incident up as an 'Idiot Tourist'.

Money was changing hands at Canterbury in the mid 1980s when a minor infraction of the rules escalated.

Barry Bowles was the-man-on-the-button and excluded Kelvin Mullarky for being the primary cause of a stoppage. Kelvin didn't like the decision and came to the referees box to argue how Barry was wrong. Not getting the decision changed Kelvin left the box and strode out onto the centre green, right in front of the referee's box, where he began to bow with up-stretched arms as if in mock worship. The crowd loved it but, of course, Barry had to fine him. This upset his promoter Wally Maudsley who ran over to join Kelvin and his rant was not as polite as Kelvin's had been. This instigated an instant fine for Wally, which caused Wally to incite the crowd, working them up into a right old frenzy – another fine.

During the tirade Wally took out his wallet and pulled out a note, which he gave to Kelvin with overacted gestures and theatrics, for Kelvin to pay his fine. This meant yet another fine, this time the maximum and a report to the Speedway Control Board.

But as referee Bowles recalled: *'The last laugh was on Wally anyway because a few weeks later Kelvin was laughing about the incident, in which he bore no malice because he was not that kind of man. The reason for the laughter was that in the heat of the moment Wally had given Kelvin a £50 note and Kelvin's fine was only £10!*

The outcome of the SCB Tribunal was that Wally Maudsley received a hefty fine in addition to the £50 I had imposed and he was banned from speedway tracks, including Canterbury, for quite a period of time.

This was particularly hard on him because he was England Team manager at the time.

As the 1978 season drew to a close there were seven claimants for the Scunthorpe's track record of 76.8 around the Quibble Park raceway. They were headed by Saints skipper Keith Evans who held it unopposed for eighteen months before Phil Collins and John Jackson grabbed a share about a year later then, Kelvin Malarkey, Phil White, Nicky Allot and Bob Garret joined the fray and all on the same night.

Secretary of the Association of referees Dave Dowling says that fans have the wrong idea of a referee's role.

He says: *'Most seem to think that we just travel around the area where we live, a mile or two here and there, but most of us travel the length and breath of the country and even abroad. I could get a call at maybe 11am to say a referee is indisposed and I'm required at Poole or somewhere like that, miles away.*

A referee friend of mine who keeps a log, clocked up 9,000 miles last season!'

In the first ever speedway world final (Wembley 1936) eventual winner Australian Lionel Van Praag had to beat British rider Eric Langton in a run-off before becoming the first world champion. This despite the fact that another Australian, Bluey Wilkinson. had won all of his races and had beaten both Van Pragg and Langton in the process.

The addition of bonus points, that had been in operation throughout the qualifying rounds and added to the result on the night, meant that Wilkinson had to be content with third place.

Ron Mason, had a knack of recalling segments of his career by other grand events that happened at the same time. Ron, who would later find fame with Belle Vue, said: *'I started in speedway in 1932. I remember the year well because the following year Bluey Wilkinson won the World Championship.'*

Later during a winter tour of Australia and New Zealand, Belle Vue team regular Ron couldn't help but notice the talent of a local lad by the name of Ron Johnson. Mason said: *'He was getting by on a shoestring but he showed great talent for the sport. So Jack Parker and I carried a blanket round the track for a collection for him at a track in New Zealand and the generous Kiwi fans chipped in enough to buy Johnno a bike and a ticket to England. – again I recall the year, it was the same year that Ronnie Moore first arrived in this country.'*

39

Slovenia finished last in event two of the 2009 World Cup at Peterborough with 13 points, and captain Matej Zagar scored them all except three – and one of those was a free gift courtesy of a three-man last race. This feat he achieved despite two non-finishes – a starting gate exclusion in one start and a puncture in another.

After England suffered a twenty-six points defeat in a test match against Australia at Wembley on May 24, 1949, a match report declared: 'It was a sad reflection on the England team that a reserve rider, Freddie Williams of Wembley, who was making his first test appearance, should not only top score for his side but be outstanding as one of the few men to show fighting spirit from behind.'

A year later Freddie was world champion.

Glasgow high flying tiger Kenny McKinna received a late Christmas present for 1980 – the Scottish Junior Championship Trophy – despite having won it three months earlier. But the Glasgow Supporters Club, who own and present the trophy annually, couldn't find it when presentation time came around.

The previous year's winner, Bill Logan, couldn't shed any light on the mystery of the missing silverware having never set eyes on it during his reign as champ. A lot of head scratching and delving through old records revealed that the trophy had gone missing during his predecessor's term as champion.

It was eventually located and returned to its rightful owners who inscribed the absent names and belatedly presented it to McKinna in the middle of January.

Stoke Potters were at the seaside to race against the Yarmouth Bloaters in the summer of 1952 when the Potters speedster Ron Peace got into trouble with the local law for illegal parking.

That turned out to be bad luck for Ron because he had left his team captain Ken Adams to park the car, while he went for a paddle in the sea.

When Bradford's Odsal Stadium opened for business in June 1945, the first recorded race time was 86.8 seconds. Eight years later, almost to the day, in June 1952, Bradford's tearaway teenager Arthur Wright set a new track record of 63.2 seconds – an incredible 23.6 seconds off the old record in just eight years.

For the 1952 season, Bill Gilbert, a former West Ham and Wembley stalwart, was persuaded out of retirement to join the Norwich team.

The white line expert joined forces with Stars rider Fred Pawson as heat partner and the pair became a first class team-riding combination. So much so that they waltzed away with the top prize in a Best Pairs competition held later in the year at Norwich.

Ted Bravery, Norwich stalwart 1946 to 1950, with Wally Lloyd and treasurer Sid Singleton, formed the Riders Benevolent Fund on September 26, 1947. The three Speedway Riders Association members announced that the kitty amounted to £5,467 7s 5d, collected from contributions, dances etc.

So says three time world champion Ole Olsen, *'Engine power alone is not enough; there is still a place for skill and track craft.'* And who could argue with that?

The legendary Jack Parker was among the first people in England to try his hand at speedway when he took to the track at Kings Oak over the Witsun weekend, 1928.

Former world champion Greg Hancock is the only rider to have qualified for and raced in every Grand Prix since the competition inception in 1995. 'American' Greg was world champion in 1997. To date, at the end of the 2009 campaign, Hancock has raced in every one of the 122 Grands Prix, winning ten of them and reaching the final an incredible forty-nine times. Along the way he collected 1533 points from his 666 GP rides – which included 224 GP heat wins.

Speedway's first English world champion, Tommy Price, also rode on the tarmac. He once raced against the well remembered first class tarmac specialist, Geoff Duke, at Silverstone. He also competed at Brands Hatch, Oulton Park and Snetterton, among others. He rode in the 1957 Isle of Man Manx Grand Prix. His last time on the tarmac was in the Hutchinson100 at Silverstone. He said: *'The reason you may not have seen my name in the programmes etc, is because I always called myself TH Price on the road circuits. I did that deliberately so people wouldn't know I was Tommy Price and expect great things from me.'*

At the end of the 1950s a track was laid under the Chiswick flyover, in London. It became the home base of the Southern Area League team the Chiswick Nomads. The tiny circuit was only about half the length of most other tracks at 200 yards.

Founder–rider was Ted Payne and other team members were Arthur Ashby, Dave Freeborn, Roy Pickering, Pete Rogers, Bill Pittingale and Eric Jolly.

Speedway rider Jack Parker really was a legend in his own lifetime. He was known – and quite rightly so – as *'the best rider never to win the world championship'*. Ron Mason, Jack's long time riding partner, had nothing but praise for his team captain and pal.

'Jack would put the bike where he wanted it to be,' he said. *'In fact Jack could put his front wheel right up against your leg without actually touching you and that was very often enough to unnerve members of the opposing team.'*

The Latvian round of the 2009 Grand Prix was a very close fought contest in Daugavpils on August 1. So much so that the first ten races had ten different winners.

Eventual meeting winner American Greg Hancock, spoilt the run by taking heat eleven, his second win of the night.

July 7, 1994 is a day that will live in infamy in speedway circles for a very long time.

It was heat 14 at Ipswich and Mitch Shirra failed to make the two minutes and accordingly was excluded. Barry Bowles was the referee and he says that what happened next was shameful.

'Shirra managed to get from the pits to my box,' he recalls. *'The first I knew was hearing the door being kicked in. The door was always locked but the doorframe was smashed and the door flew open. Within a moment I had a great pain in my right ear and I felt myself plunging to the floor off my stool. Shirra had hold of my ear and was shouting obscenities at me and in front of the startled announcer, timekeeper and my wife, who always acted as my scribe, filling in the five programmes that I was obliged to complete. He was overpowered and removed from the box.*

Shirra was fined £10 for unauthorised approach to a referee (SR176f) and the maximum £50 for dissent (SR176e), and I also reported the incident to the Speedway Control Board.

At the subsequent SCB Tribunal, during which he also kicked the SCB solicitor, Mitch Shirra was banned from the sport and had to pay a hefty fine.'

For his first ever race at West Ham, Tommy Miller had the unnerving experience of watching the nuts holding his front wheel on slowly undo.

Riding in Scotland's colours Tommy had to make a quick decision – to keep going or pull up. He decided to take a chance and it paid off – just.

Returning to the pits after the race both nuts were so loose that they fell off.

Jack Parker with Ron Mason on the outside ~ Belle Vue, 1949

World champion in-waiting, Ove Fundin, was signed by Norwich in June 1955 and scored eight points in his first meeting for the Stars. Later, as a reserve, he had four rides against Birmingham and won them all. A sign of things to come.

Danny Dunton was a useful team member with Harringay, and second only to Vic Duggan in popularity around the London raceway. But Danny had a second and less auspicious claim to fame: during his racing career he rode in the colours of Yarmouth, Weymouth and Bristol as well as Harringay – and each track closed down while he was on their books.

It has long been bandied about that the first person to come up with a foolproof method of securing the helmet cover so that it doesn't come adrift during the course of the race, could well add considerably to their pension fund. But in recent times most riders in the upper echelon have arrived at their own solution – they have four helmets, one of each colour.

Apart from international matches where all four colours would be required, they only need to take two to domestic league meetings: the red and blue ones for home meetings and the other two: white and yellow when they travel away.

But it appears that none of them are prepared to speculate in one more, this time coloured black and white – in case they need it once in a while.

Mike Broadbanks, long time Swindon shale shifter was one of the last riders to use the old JAP engines. He said: *'When I first started riding, first at Rye House and then Wembley, there was nothing else. Then when I joined Swindon everyone was telling me to swop over to ESO which had taken over as the main engine, but I was beating all of them anyway,'*

Later the JAWA came on the scene but by then Mike was well established with his JAP and stayed with his decision. By then he says, with so many people changing away from JAP engines, he was able to get very substantial discounts for spares. Plus, he added: *'I was still earning as much as the others, so why would I feel I had to change.'*

Welshman Freddie Williams was second only to his team captain Tommy Price in the points table with 1854 points from 237 matches. But Freddie who rode one year less, 1947 to 1956, had one claim to fame that even his high-flying captain couldn't better.

In 1953, as reigning world champion, Freddie set a new track record at Wembley – but this Wembley was in Johannesburg, South Africa.

1951, the year that Aussie Jack Young took the world championship title for the first time, he was almost unstoppable. He started the season by recording eleven successive maximums. He dropped a mere couple of points, then back on the winning trail he notched up a further eight successive maximums. A couple of more points dropped in his next meeting then he chipped in with a further six maximums on the trot.

That year Jack finished with an almost unbelievable average of 11.7.

Tommy Price rode in all eleven post war seasons for Wembley, 1946 to 1956, and never once lost his heat leader status. Throughout that period he amassed a total of 2,403 points from 287 matches, which naturally made him the team's top points scorer.

When Ken McKinlay began his speedway career in 1948 at Glasgow White City his debut was less than sensational. For the first two years he was in and out of the team so much that it was a wonder he was not called Yo-Yo McKinlay. So many things happened to Ken and his bike in his early days, including his chain breaking at the starting gate and slicing the tapes in half, that he acquired the name of 'Voodoo' McKinlay.

But by 1953 he had earned the much more popular name of Hurri-Ken, a name that stuck with him for the remainder of his twenty seven years in the sport.

In 1970 at Newcastle, with more than twenty years in the saddle, Ken scored an impeccable eighteen point maximum for Scotland against England in an international match. No other Scot had ever scored a maximum for his country in England before.

1978 was an history making year for speedway because it was the sport's Golden Jubilee year. It was also a ground breaking year for Crayford speedway for it was on Tuesday September 19 that year that they came up with a first for speedway when they invited the four Collins brothers to compete as a team in a four team tournament.

For the first time the four brothers, Peter, Phil, Les and younger brother Neil came together as one team to compete against a home squad of Kestrels, plus quartets from Hackney and Wimbledon. The Collins family kept it in the family by drafting in mum, Mrs Eileen Collins, as team manager.

Crayford promoter Peter Throrogood said: *'Tonight we witness a worldwide first. I'm amazed that no-one had ever thought of bringing the four Collins boys together before!'*

When former Boston rider Robert Mouncer decided to try his hand in the German League with Diedenbergen, he was pleasantly surprised to find that things worked differently over there. His promoters found him and his wife a flat and Robert a job, as required by German law. He said: *'Over there they were prepared to help you out. I was on a retainer plus points money and that will add up to as much as if I cleaned up in the First Division in England.'*

Philip Morris has been on five television quiz shows, with two of them making him a nice little nest egg – and not so little at that.

The Colour of Money on ITV with Chris Tarrant netted Philip £63,000, and *Are You Smarter than a Ten Year Old* with hosts Dick and Dom, brought in a further £25,000.

He said: *'They were great days out and I would advise everyone to try and get on a game show.'*

In the June 1949 edition of East Anglian Speedway, a monthly magazine, under the heading of *'East Anglians to the fore'* was the prophetic gem: *'... closer to home we have two East Anglian forecasts as the most improved riders of their respective divisions, Paddy Mills of Norwich, and wee Billy Bales of Yarmouth who shook them all by his brilliance in the championship of the world meeting at Sheffield.'*

Fifteen years later upon Norwich's closure Bales was transferred to Sheffield where in his first meeting for his new club Billy was unbeaten by an opposing rider to finish the night with a paid maximum.

Bill Kitchen, captain of Wembley Lions, was asked to write about the basics of speedway for a schoolboys magazine in 1952. This is his appraisal:

'Getting round corners at speed on a fast machine, without brakes, on a 400 yards circuit is the speedway riders basic problem and the crowds delight. The modern broadsiding technique is to drive into a controlled skid at 40 mph, holding the front wheel steady by bringing the left leg forward, arms steering, while the right hand manipulates the throttle control. The abandoned broadside, with both wheels sliding on the loose surface and left leg trailing is more spectacular but generally less effective than the steady slide at half throttle, corrected at the vital second by opening out at full speed.

Races are won and lost on the bends and this is where you take the most risks, so riders wear padded riding kit, heavy boots and helmet.'

Rob Mouncer

Eastbourne's Steve Weatherley was pleased when his turn at a jaunt at the Silver Helmet Match Race title came up although he was up against the almost invincible Joey Owen.

Owen beat Weatherley in two straight legs at Eastbourne in a prelude to the Eastbourne v Newcastle match, leaving young Steve to reflect on what might have been. *'Joe beat me in the races for the Helmet before the match, then I went out and beat him in the races where we met in the match,'* he said ruefully. 'Maybe it was nerves, that got to me where I wanted to beat him in front of my home fans, made me miss the gate when it really mattered.'

Not often do you see four attempts to finish a particular heat, especially at world level. But that's what happened for an epic heat 12 of the 2009 Nordic Grand Prix round at Vojens on August 29.

On a night when rain threatened continually and everyone wanted to get finished before the heavens opened, it took four attempts before eventually getting a result.

As the four riders lined up at the gate there was movement as the tapes rose, occasioning a restart with all four. The second time they got away in fine style but the race was stopped again when American Greg Hancock was excluded for bringing down Polish rider Tomasz Gollop while they were engaged in an elbow-to-elbow tussle. The third time it was Gollop himself that was excluded when he was nudged over to the fence bringing down fellow Pole Rune Holta in the process.

Heat 12 of the eighth round of the 2009 Grand Prix eventually got completed at the fourth attempt with the remaining two riders only, where Holta led Swede Fredrik Lindgren from gate to flag.

Kings Lynn flyer David Gagen was guest of honour at the grand opening of Radio Rentals, TV retailers, new premises in Kings Lynn. The former Junior Championship finalist cracked: 'This is one way to get on television.'

Talk about drink-driving!
Former world champion and soon-to-be world champion again Ivan Mauger, signed up a splendid sponsorship deal with Ricard, the French aperitif manufacturers, in April 1976 and, although it was April, it was no April Fool's joke. The quadruple world champ was kitted out with new Ricard leathers, bike covers, and other goodies, estimated to be part of a package worth at least three thousand pounds.

It is not too common an occurrence but it does happen once in a while that a rider has to 'free-wheel' the last few yards to collect the final point after an engine failure in a three man finish, and every now and then a rider might have to push his bike home for the same reason. But Cradley Heathens experience takes some beating – and stamina from the riders.

On October 1, 1977 in a late season match against Hull, two riders were excluded for various reasons and the remaining pair had engine failures in the re-run and were obliged to push home for the points.

One pushed his bike for a full lap which was quite a feat in itself but the other one had further to go because his bike had packed up half a lap earlier.

Young Dane Leon Madsen celebrated his first ever speedway win on August 3, 2009.

In a Poole v Coventry meeting Madsen started ff the night with a third place, which was followed by two last places, before powering his way to his first chequered flag in heat twelve, his ast race of the night. In what could have been a fairytale race, the kind that dreams are made of, it would have put the icing on the cake if Leon had led his partner home for the epoch making 5-1 win but it was not to be. However, his partner gave his best try to pick up the last point giving the Poole pairing a 4-2 heat victory.

A broken ankle looked like Sunderland's Jack Millen would be out of action for some time. But no, 'Millen the Villain', as he was known, arrived for the next meeting with a plaster cast on his left leg and proceeded to strap on the largest steel boot one could imagine. It resembled a barge in size yet didn't affect his performance at all.

Six times British Youth Grasstrack Champion, Philip Morris, after turning to speedway, helped to make a documentary for Channel 4 in 2000. It was mainly about Reading speedway. He designed the Reading Euphony team suit in 2004 and was also 50% shareholder in the Reading track shop in 2004 and 2005.

In 1937 American Minty Wain arrived in England to join Wimbledon for the start of the league season. Although at 37 he was old by today's standards Wain arrived with an impressive pedigree, having won almost everything there was to win on the other side of the Atlantic. He was also an accomplished *Wall-of-Death* performer.

Minty suffered a broken left leg that put him in hospital and, upon his discharge, he found that leg was shorter than the other one. Soon after he crashed again and this time he broke the other leg. When the plaster was removed from his right leg he found that both legs were the same length again.

Former world champion Ronnie Moore started his two-wheel career and subsequent rise to the pinnacle of the speedway world as a pillion rider!

His father Les Moore, a *Wall-of-Death* rider with his own show in Australia, took a twelve-year-old Ronnie for a spin around the wall on his pillion. Later Ronnie became a wall rider himself and toured New Zealand with his father and the show.

Ronnie came to England with Norman Parker in 1950 and was introduced to Wimbledon. Before the season's end he had become a first class rider in Division One, before going on to World honours in 1954.

Ronnie stayed in the sport for almost twenty-five years until a serious crash in Australia in 1975 put paid to a brilliant career.

Somewhere along his long reign on the shale Olle Nygren picked the Swedish title of Varg Olle. Olle explained that Varg means wolf in Swedish.

Many would say that maybe it was a bit much sticking dear old Olle with such a fierce name with all its implications. Always a competitive rider and mostly a fair adversary, perhaps likening him to a wolf was going a bit too far.

During his stint as a training school instructor, at his world renowned training sessions over many years, Olle had been known to get a bit hot under the collar with some trainees that were a bit slow on the uptake, although it was never recorded that he actually took a bite out of anyone.

For the England v Australasia Test Match held at Norwich on August 5, 1955 both opposing team captains were Norwich riders. Billy Bales captained the England team and his domestic teammate Aub Lawson skippered the squad from down under.

Bales was top scorer for England, powering to 13 points while Lawson managed four for the Kangaroos and Kiwis. There were two other Norwich riders in the England team, Cyril Roger and Norwich captain Phil Clarke who both weighed in with useful points to help the home team win the Test by 57 to 51.

Later that year that same Norwich trio of Bales, Clarke and Roger were at it again in the World Championship Final at Wembley and had the added bonus of being joined by new Norwich signing Ove Fundin.

Ronnie Moore and Barry Briggs

During his twenty-eight year career in British speedway, Swede Olle Nygren, donned the body colours of ten different clubs. They were Bristol, Coventry, Harringay, Ipswich, Kings Lynn, Norwich, Southampton, Swindon, West Ham and Wimbledon.

Multiple speedway world championship winner, Swede Ove Fundin, finished last in his first world final in 1954. He then went on to win the crown in 1956, 1960, 1961, 1963 and 1967. For the years in between he made his presence felt with ten points in 1955 and then second place in 1957, 1958 and 1959. Third places followed in 1962, 1964 and 1965 before bowing out in 1968 and 1969 with seven and nine points respectively

---

The 1978 saw the two Match Race Helmets, Gold and Silver, in safekeeping throughout the entire season.

With Peter Collins starting the season as holder of the Golden Helmet and brushing aside all challengers to end up still retaining the shiny skid lid at the season end; with Tom Owen doing likewise with the National League's Silver version. Owen didn't start off as holder as Collins had done but took the title and the trophy in the first clash of the season by beating Bob Coles for the vacant possession.

Tom Owen's grip on the Silver Helmet Match Race title could not be broken by challengers that came at him from the length and breadth of the country, instead it fell to a break of a different kind. After almost two seasons, 1978 and 1979, Tom finally had to admit defeat to, of all things, a broken leg.

World champion Jack Young turned up to ride at Wimbledon only to find that he wasn't expected and therefore no rides were available. So, changing back out of his leathers, 'Aussie' Jack had visions of a night off only to find that he had to stay because he couldn't get his car out of the car park.

Paddy Mills, hard riding Norwich team member when speedway resumed after World War Two, was the first second division rider to be capped to ride for England in a Test Match.

Thirty years later, another rider from the same part of the country, Kings Lynn rider, Michael Lee, was at the time believed to be the youngest rider ever capped for the England squad.

George Newton sidelined two of his own Harringay team members at the start of the 1937 season. He managed to knock off Bill Pritcher and Norman Parker over the same weekend. Both suffered broken arms.

At the rebirth of speedway in 1946 after World War Two, Tommy Price renewed his association with Wembley. He started with a bang by winning the British Riders Championship and was handed the captaincy of the Lions

Tommy established himself as the team's top points scorer and, throughout the eleven seasons of operations until the Lions demise in 1956, he never once lost his heat leader position.

The long arm of the law stretched even further on Saturday July 4, 2009 when Berwick Speedway received a visit from the boys in blue.

PC Paul Temple and his colleague from Northumbrian Traffic Police were invited to bring their sophisticated laser speed gun equipment to record the speed of the riders in that night's meeting at Sheilfield Park.

The bandits were entertaining Newport Wasps in a Premier League meeting and the fastest speed of the night went to visitors captain Paul Fry. Fry was clocked at an incredible 75 mph down the fastest part of the 368 metre circuits back straight.

During an away match against Lakeside Hammers, Poole's high flying Swede Bjarne Pedersen enlightened us with the gem: *'It's hard to slow down and keep up your speed.'*

A classic that may go down in the annals of speedway history? Maybe there is something lost in translation from Swedish into English.

Swede Ove Fundin certainly made speedway history in 1967 when he raced to an unprecedented fifth world championship win. But the very next year, New Zealander Ivan Mauger embarked upon his epic journey that would lead him to a record six wins over the next eleven years: 1968 1969, 1970, 1972, 1977, 1979.

When Norwich closed down at the end of 1964 season Billy Bales was transferred to Sheffield, and in his first meeting for his new club, in May 1965, Billy weighed in with a paid maximum to help in the Tigers win over Exeter.

Jack Young had his first meeting in this country for Edinburgh on April 2, 1949. 'Aussie' Jack set a new track record and scored a maximum in that first match and left the Monarchs fans a strong indication of what was in store for them.

Young finished his first season as he had began it; he won the Scottish Match Race Title and finished the season at the top of his clubs averages with a total of 278 points.

Reading racer Dave Jessup tried to keep in shape over the close season by playing golf and by riding trials. In 1978 he was given a nice Christmas present, a brand new 350cc Bultaco, by near neighbour to his Kent home, Norman Flurry of Watling Tyres. Dave celebrated by cleaning a pile of old tyres outside the service station before going onto the real thing on Boxing Day in the Medway MCC trial.

Dave also learned to play golf by starting on a practice range and over the years has become a first class player to such an extent that presumably his earnings from a little white ball and a set of clubs keep him in the lifestyle that he became accustomed to with a bike and lots of shale shifting.

Kelvin Tatum, later to talk sense as a TV speedway commentator, was England's only representative for the 1985 world final. He finished the night in eighth place with eight points. Phil Collins also qualified as second reserve but didn't get a ride.

Arriving at Barrow for the first time ever was daunting as the track was built around a football pitch. One bend was round and normal, but the other consisted of a sharp left turn, a short but definite straight section, then another sharp bend to exit. The boarding, safety fence, went straight across this bend so there was no question of a rider trying to make a round turn instead of two definite ones. On this particular day there was a large wet patch of mud on the entry. Quite clearly it would be impossible to enter this bend sideways, which was imperative. The home riders were equally concerned about the situation and asked George Barclay if he could have a word with the promoter and referee in his position as SRA secretary. The promoter understood and said he would leave a decision to the referee.

Realising that the adjudicator was not keen to call the meeting off, George said, 'If this was first division the riders would not agree to ride.' To which the referee replied, 'But George, if this was first division they would not be expected to ride.'

Billy Bales, long time shale shifter with Norwich Stars, called his eldest son Raymond although he didn't use the name himself. Billy was christened Raymond Arthur Bales.

White Liners

Well-remembered professional wrestler, Jackie Pallo, *'the man we loved to hate'* who graced the rings and television screens during the 1960s and 1970s, was no stranger to a speedway bike.

Jackie had several tryouts and practices with the Wembley Lions team at their training base Rye House. He said that he loved the sport and would have liked to have become better acquainted and more proficient at it, maybe even looking for a team place. Unfortunately he was advised against taking it any further, *'I was just beginning to make my name in wrestling at that time,'* he said, *'and to have injured myself would have knocked me out of both sports.'*

Speedway's loss was certainly wrestling's gain.

Speedway

After a long and illustrious career on the shale, Belle Vue's stalwart Ron Mason turned to a different kind of horsepower. Ron replaced shale for grass as a racehorse owner and trainer. Notforsaking his speedway connections entirely, he named his first horse *'Fuel'*. But Ron's great success came from his appropriately named horse *'Track Spare'*, who won the1966 St James's Palace Stakes. *'Last Lap'*, *'First Bend'* and *'Chequered Flag'*, also featured prominently in his stable.

Speedway

During the war years Wembley's Tommy Price served with the American Airborne Division.

Speedway

Norwich rider Harry Edwards was a Japanese prisoner of war before being repatriated. He took up speedway and stayed in the sport for more than ten years.

Speedway

Speedway rider Kiwi Bill Andrews knew all about horsepower and how to stay in the saddle because he was also a licensed jockey. Bill, a National Hunt (over the sticks) jockey, retired from horse racing in 1971 to concentrate fully on speedway.

Another mat-man of note with speedway in his blood was Bobby Ryan. Bobby won the European Lightweight Championship by defeating the title holder Jim Breaks in a televised bout at Wolverhampton on August 17, 1975. But even then still maintained that his first love was speedway.

Bobby first got the speedway bug when he was ten years old. *'My uncle, himself a keen speedway fan, owned a farm and he allowed me a bit of land to lay myself some sort of a track,'* he said.

After laying tons of shale, he bought an old BSA 500 road bike which he stripped down and raced around his home made track until police turned up and closed him down on the grounds of noise, which could be heard a mile away. Not to be deterred, he bought a 'proper bike' as he called it and was accepted for training with Dent Oliver at Belle Vue.

At that stage his father, Stan Rylands, a wrestling referee, persuaded young Bobby to try his hand at wrestling, hoping that he would forget speedway and probably in time forget wrestling as well. Bobby recalls: *'My father never wanted me to wrestle; it was just a trick to get me away from speedway. But I made the grade in wrestling and have made numerous television appearance – but I still get the urge to jump on a speedway bike!'*

Andy Ross was a trackman that had successful shale and ice-racing career before changing to a different kind of horsepower, and in his case power meant just that. The Peterborough skipper of the 1970s owned Brookfield Shires, a Shire horse stable and stud farm at Alconbury Weston in Huntington, where he displayed around forty of the enormous animals very successfully at shows up and down the country, including the East of England Showground where his shale career was established.

Halifax rider of the mid 1970s Ian Cartwright is a member of the Robert Thompsons furniture makers family. Ian, a carpenter and cabinetmaker works for the firm that were known for the little mouse carved into their furniture.

Berwick's track record is the longest surviving in speedway and has stood the test of time (and riders) for a decade. Sheffield's Sean Wilson set the fastest time of all time at 64.2 ten years ago and since then no one has been able to surpass that feat.

Peter Craven,
World Champion 1955 and 1962

Norwich Stars middle order man, Ted Bravery, was being dubbed *'The old Fella'* as long ago as June 1949.

Ian Hoskins went on a speedway fact-finding trip to Majorca in 1971 and with him was Wimbledon whiz kid Reg Luckhurst. They got involved with the San Pardo circuit in Palma, where Reg, due to his inventor's spirit, coupled with being a first class engineer, made a track grader out of old bits found around the place. He also improvised a water cart from the chassis of an old Comer van and a petrol tank.

Max Rech, St Austell's Polish rider of the early 1950s was a fighter pilot during the World War Two.

After his serious crash in 1957, Swindon's Bob Roger was in hospital for quite some time with complete loss of memory. His accident wiped out the memory of more than two years of Bob's life. He says he vaguely recalls people standing round his bedside as visitors and when they left he got up and walked out with them – not just once but on several occasions. *'Several times, so I'm told, the staff found me way up the road wandering off, still in my pyjamas.'*

A professional mat man who preferred the wide open spaces of speedway to the close contact of professional Greco-Roman wrestling was Soren Sjosten. The Belle Vue speedster started his wrestling career in 1956 and perfected his first choice of sport whilst serving in the Swedish navy, where he won the Marine Swedish Wrestling Championship at flyweight.

After demob he turned his hand to the shale scene in his native Sweden and progressed enough to clinch a team place in the Aces line-up in 1967.

When Martyn Piddock won the Kent Messenger Trophy, a Kent newspaper sponsored annual meeting at Canterbury, on September 29, 1969 it was the fourth match that he had competed in that day.

Busy Martyn started the day at Rayleigh as a Canterbury rider in a four-team tournament. That afternoon he helped West Ham in a Division One double-header against Coatbridge and then Kings Lynn. He then travelled to Canterbury to contest his fourth match of the day – and pick up that Kent Messenger Trophy.

Speedway

Tommy Price first rode for Wembley in 1935 – Lionel van Praag was captain.

Speedway

The original starting gate was invented by Fred Monkford in 1932 and put into use at New Cross. When New Cross shut up shop that same gate went on its travels until in 1968, when Canterbury opened for business, it was installed at the home of the Crusaders. Then, when the Kingsmead Stadium ceased operating for speedway, that gate had been in continuous operation for almost fifty years.

Speedway

Prior to the introduction of Kevlars, a well made set of racing leathers would need up to three miles of thread for stitching.

Speedway

During 1971–1972 Reg Luckhurst tried his hand at coaching in Majorca and is credited with teaching a score of Spaniards how to ride speedway. The long time Wimbledon rider designed his own speedway frames and built his own bikes. With Ian Hoskins as promoter the pair of them put on an entire twenty-heat meeting in Palma with only five bikes in working order – the same bikes appearing in every race. They later claimed this as a world record.

Speedway

Billy Bolton, a boxer of the 1930s, boxed successfully with the handicap of an artificial leg, and while speedway can't match that, there has been the odd occasion when a speedway rider has defied the odds to ride with disabilities that would lay mere mortals low for a very long time, if not forever.

Many riders have been recorded over the years as riding with broken legs or arms still in plaster, and Yarmouth rider Ted Rawlinson rode in the Bloaters colours in the 1940s despite having no sight in one eye. A rider for Crayford in the days of the old Highwaymen was similarly afflicted, as was Newcastle rider Vic Lonsdale. It's not recorded how those riders lost their eye but Norfolk based Czech Tony Svab said he lost his eye whilst ice racing when his goggles came off and one of his eyes froze.

There was also Eric Peacock the trick motorcyclist of the 1930s, who did stunt trick riding on the centre green to entertain the crowds despite having only one arm.

Speedway

Reading fans witnessed the youngest ever motorcycle stunt rider in May 1980 at Smallmead Stadium, when seven-year-old Darius Goodwin entertained them from the centre green. At one stage young Darius jumped his bike over all eight of the Racers team.

Speedway

Fay Taylor was the first recognised lady speedway rider of any substance; Eva Asquith started around the same time and also was fast becoming a force to be reckoned with. Fay learned her basic craft at Crystal Palace and Eva did likewise in the northern counties. With others they travelled to Australia in 1928 where those two, and in particular Fay Taylor, held their own against the top riders of the time. They went out again in 1929 and after a few races found that a new ban had been instituted banning lady riders. Upon returning home they found that the ban applied in England as well.

It was rumoured that both these lady riders always raced with pyjamas under their leathers – in case of having to go to hospital.

Speedway

To start the 1977 campaign, Reading rider Dave Jessup sported a brand new set of leathers that had been designed by the Reading fans. Around 60 fans entered a competition and Dave gave the winning design an airing around the Reading raceway.

Speedway

The 1984 Northern Riders Final at Halifax became the Collins Carnival when three Collins boys took the three top places. Belle Vue's Peter mounted the winners rostrum, having scored 14 points, Sheffield's brother Les was second with 13 and Tiger's team mate Neil completed the trio by claiming third place with 11 points.

Another brother, Phil, was busy at the same time with his team Cradley and yet one more brother, Stephen was away learning the broadsiding art with Arena Essex.

contribution he was on the losing team. Nevertheless, while the winning team received up a trophy apiece, young Mr Howe picked up two – one for his maximum and one for the fastest time of the meeting.

Speedway

Eastbourne's Steve Weatherley recalled his first handicap but it wasn't on the track, it was in the classroom. *'In my first season, having just turned sixteen, I had made it to a team place and was riding at number seven.'* he said. *'In my first ever away match, we were at Crewe and I fell off and broke my collarbone in my first race. I was still at school and taking my exams. Back at school and in the exam room I must have looked a bit strange because I couldn't move my arm to write so I had to move the paper instead.'*

Speedway

Leicester Lions got into the Guinness Book of Records when in 1969 they fielded the same seven rider team for the entire season. Wolverhampton almost equalled that record in 2009 but they required eight riders to do so after a member of the main team was injured. On the other hand, Swindon failed to win even one away match during 1975.

Speedway

Aussie Harry Denton must qualify as the oldest speedway 'junior' of all time. When Northampton's Brafield reopened for speedway in 1966 after a ten year absence from the shale scene, they launched their new opening with a Junior Riders Championship and Denton was one of the competitors – Harry was 51 at the time.

Speedway

Eric Boocock was the first rider to be awarded a testimonial meeting. This took place at Halifax in 1974. Eric said: *'We attracted the biggest crowd since Manchester United played there.'*

As this was the first ever testimonial, the promotion had no precedent and had not thought it through fully. If Eric was rubbing his hands with glee, his euphoria was short lived when he was told he was sharing his big moment with two others and the proceeds would have to be shared three ways.

Speedway

Entertainer Freddie Starr read of Ipswich teamster Tony Davey's lack of funds so he bought Davey a new bike although the couple had never met.

In July 1978 Davey was reported in the newspapers as being in dire financial straits and was contemplating selling his car in order to continue racing. When TV funny man Starr read of Davey's dilemma he immediately sent him a £1000 cheque. Davey was able to order a brand new Weslake bike just in time to for him to compete in the Daily Mirror sponsored Grand Prix at London's White City where his new bike carried him to a creditable fourth place and a prize of £350.

In 1999 Mark Loram was the first rider in Grand Prix history to win a GP as a wild card entry. A year later, 2000, Mark was the only rider to make all six semi-finals and secure enough points to win the World championship.

When former world champion Ronnie Moore was disqualified for breaking the tapes in a heat of the Manpower Trophy meeting at Reading in 1971, he told everyone and anyone who would listen that it was the first time that he had been excluded for breaking the tapes in over twenty years.

The 1937 world final, held at Wembley, the first three places went to Americans. Jack Milne took the title closely followed by Wilbur Lamoreaux, with Jack's brother Cordy Milne making it a clean sweep.

At his retirement from the shale in 2009, Philip Morris had been Wales No.1 rider for seventeen years. He was the first ever speedway rider to test the track at the Millennium Stadium, prior to the GPs being staged there. Philip was asked to do some PR work and came up with valuable feedback on what he thought of the track, which helped to get things ironed out in advance of the super Millennium Grand Prix. He said: *'I go to the stadium to watch Wales play football and the rugby so to be invited to ply my trade in that same venue left me feeling a bit overawed and it took me a few laps to come to terms with it all.'*

In 1964, after a nine-year layoff and with speedway in the doldrums, West Ham were persuaded to reopen to make racing viable with seven tracks operating. This they did in front of 15,000 fans.

They were managed by former world champion Tommy Price and led by soon-to-be world champion Bjorn Knutsson, The team managed to finish the season propping up the other six teams in the National League. The next year was a different story. With the formation of the British League and captained by Ken McKinlay they took the new league title.

The Wembley Lions, under the leadership of Tommy Price, were league champions seven out of the first eight seasons. The remainder they finished second twice and third once. The only time they slipped up was 1948 when the Olympics required their home stadium and the Lions were obliged to race all their home matches at Wimbledon.

Graham Miles recalls what he calls 'a disastrous night'. It happened on July 17, 1971 whilst riding for Hackney in a double-header against Sheffield and Kings Lynn. Graham had only fallen off once previously that season but things were to change on 'his disastrous night'.

It started with his first ride in the Sheffield match when he came off and broke his foot, but he persevered, came last in his next ride and won his last. Then during the Kings Lynn match he suffered his third fall of the year followed by another last place. Then, in his third ride he picked up the dirt around the outside of the Kings Lynn pair of Terry Betts and Malcolm Simmons and was thrown off, over the fence and head first into the iron crash barrier. In that moment he suffered an horrific crash that put him hospital for several months with seven broken ribs; his eighth ninth and eleventh dorsal vertebra, a fractured sternum and a punctured lung, plus concussion that he suffered for eight weeks – and the previously broken foot. On top of that a blood clot brought on a heart attack six weeks later just as things were beginning to improve. The whole episode left Graham in a wheelchair. It really was *a disastrous night*.

Jack Parker started his two-wheeled career as a trials rider with BSA. During his spell with BSA, in 1928, Jack designed and built the first ever purpose made speedway bike which, with a few minor refinements, was produced by the BSA factory. The company had their own testing track in the factory grounds and part of Jack's job was to track test every machine before it left the premises.

For his first world championship win, in 1951, as an Edinburgh rider, the man from down under, Jack Young, had to fight hard to gain the laurels. Having finished the night on twelve points with two other riders, he had to contest a three man run-off and was obliged to do it the hard way, from behind.

The following year presented no real problems, for with twelve points in the bag he was content to sit in second place in his final outing, safe in the knowledge that two points would be enough to give him the coveted crown.

To celebrate the fiftieth Anniversary of Speedway in England in 1978 a brand new five-match test series was introduced and was staged during July and August. Sponsored by the London Rubber Company and known as the *'Durex England v Australasia Test Match Series'*, it pitted England's best: Malcolm Simmons, Peter Collins, Michael Lee, Dave Jessup and Gordon Kennett ; against the cream from down under: Ivan Mauger, Mitch Shirra, Larry Ross, Billy Sanders and John Boulger.

The venues were Bristol July 21, Birmingham July 24, with Ipswich, Hull and Hackney on August 10, 16 and 18 respectively.

The Anzac's won the series 3-2 but considerably more riders were utilised than the original advertised programme and the English team was decimated for the Hull leg by the British Riders Final being held on the same day which claimed all the English top men.

Durex donated considerable prize money and a winners trophy. Mr Charles Foot, President of the British Speedway Promoters Association, said: *'.... we are welcoming to our sport a sponsor who would be professional, dignified and imaginative – and reasonably generous!'*

There were eight speedway tracks operating in London in the heyday of the sport: Wimbledon (Mon), West Ham (Tues), New Cross (Wed), Wembley (Thurs), Harringay (Fri) and also Walthamstow, White City and Hackney

Long before he probably dreamed of becoming speedway World Champion, Peter Collins entered – and won – the first grass track race he ever contested. Within a couple of years Peter was the youngest rider to win the 350cc grasstrack championship.

Original line up for the first Durex sponsored England v Australasia test

LIKELY RIDERS:

ENGLAND

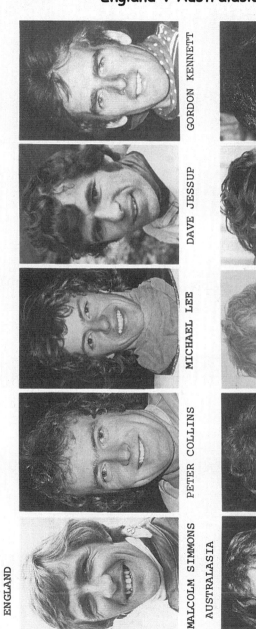

GORDON KENNETT

DAVE JESSUP

MICHAEL LEE

PETER COLLINS

MALCOLM SIMMONS

AUSTRALASIA

LARRY ROSS

MITCH SHIRRA

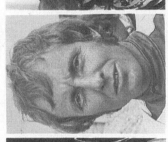

JOHN BOULGER

BILLY SANDERS

IVAN MAUGER

Photographs courtesy of Speedway Star

Olle Nygren Swedish track master who spent twenty eight years gracing British shale, started speedway in Sweden as long ago as 1947. He made his British debut at Harringay in 1951 and his World Final debut only a couple of years later in 1953. He went on to four more World Finals in 1954, 1955, 1958 and 1959. By coincidence Olle finished fourth in his first final and achieved the same position in his last. He then raced on for a further twenty years before hanging up his leathers in 1979.

Olle was also an accomplished tarmac racer. He won ten Road Racing Championships in his native Sweden and also powered to silver medals in the Isle of Man TT races.

A victim of Jason Crump late season return to 2009 British League racing with Belle Vue that caused his transfer to Swindon, Morten Risager riding at No 7 for his new team and having just won his first race said of his unwanted transfer: *'I'm not good enough to be in the team that's bottom of the league but I'm good enough to be in the team that is leading the table.'* – a bit weird.

Aussie Aub Lawson started his speedway career in 1937. He he came to England in 1939 and was signed by Wembley, who loaned him out to Middlesborough. Aub raced to the final of the world championship at the end of his first season but then he was involved in an off-track tussle with a certain Mr Hitler and was lost to speedway until 1945.

He arrived back in England in 1947 and joined West Ham. The following year he was laid low with a badly broken leg whilst competing in a Test Match at Belle Vue but still managed to finish in the top half of Division One's leading scorers.

The next year he was called up for test duty again and helped his country to victory in a Test Match raced at Birmingham and remained the Hammers loyal performer for the next couple of years before joining Norwich on loan, becoming a Stars regular in 1952.

New World Champion Olle Olsen powered himself to a superb win in the 1975 world final with a maximum at Wembley and in the process showed everyone that he was the smartest track craftsman around. Soon after saw the new World Champion competing in the Yorkshire Open meeting at Sheffield and was heading out for a deciding race run-off when his engine stopped, bringing him to a standstill as he approached the tapes – the 'smartest' new World Champion had forgotten to turn his fuel tap on!

Many a young speedway rider were old enough to ride a speedway bike when they first took up the sport, with several of them achieving national and, in some cases, world class, but not old enough to legally ride a bike on the roads, or drive a car.

Pete Jarman, well travelled shale shifter and tractor basher, started his speedway career with Eastbourne and finished years later back in the same place. Having travelled to Wolverhampton, Oxford and Cradley taking in eight Internationals along the way, 'Speedy' ended his riding days back at Eastbourne. He says: *'Charlie Duggard gave me my first rides at Eastbourne in 1959 and now, at the other end of my career and having something to offer, I'm glad of the chance to go back and give them the benefit of my experience. I've always found that the track where a rider starts his career gets all of the early days aggro and not much else, because as soon as they start to come good they move away.'*

Rye House Rockets were *hot stuff* at the beginning of the 1977 season – they had attracted the attention of a local heating company who came bearing gifts to the tune of £10,000. Included in the package was a new engine and a bike trailer apiece plus workshop facilities in part of the company's factory.

Most riders, given the option of whether to ride the first leg of Golden or Silver Helmet Match Races at home or away, usually opt for the away leg first with the thinking being that if things go wrong away from home, the home track advantage for the second leg will even things up. But long-time holder of the Golden Helmet title, Jack Parker had a different answer. When asked the home or away question, the pipe smoking speedway legend simply replied: *'I know exactly what to do – I win 'em all!'*

England International and Poole skipper Malcolm Simmons, was so annoyed with the way other riders kept picking up the worst in the newly launched Weslakes that he sent an open letter to the Motorcycle News asking everyone to stop knocking the Weslakes and give them a chance.

Simmons, a Weslake works rider, aimed his tirade mainly at Barry Briggs saying that the all British produced Weslake, although still in its infancy and is having a few teething problems, is still far faster than any JAWA that former world champion Briggs can lay his hands on.

By way of backing up his claims, Simmons points to fellow International rider Dave Jessup who won the Wimbledon Spring Classic and the Hackney Superama on a Weslake. He also top scored in the world championship quarterfinal at Poole, Simmons' home track, on a Weslake.

Simmons concludes his open letter by telling Briggs, a JAWA works rider, to stop knocking the Weslake and just admit that the Weslake is a far better engine than the JAWA, as results every night are proving.

At the last meeting to be staged at The Firs Stadium in Norwich in 1964 two riders, Derek Hewitt and Tony Childs, crashed rather spectacularly on the second bend and in the process brought down a large section of the safety fence. Possibly a foretaste of things to come in view of the fact that the place was soon to be demolished and cleared for housing. Maybe the pair were making an early bid for a job with the demolition crew.

Mildenhall's top man Ray Bales remembers his only excursion into the teaching side of the shale shifting profession. He says:

'It was a practice session at Boston and I let my 16-year-old brother-in-law try his hand. After getting him kitted out he had four or five laps to get the feel of the bike and the track, and he looked good and he said he felt confident. I gave him a few more pointers and set him off to try sliding, which naturally required a bit more power. Unfortunately by that stage of the day the shale had moved out toward the fence and, as soon as he touched it he was pulled in. His back wheel clipped the fence, lifting the bike up and throwing him off but he was trapped between the bike and the fence but the bike kept going,

pulling him along the straight, still attached, for about twenty yards or so.

Everyone on the centre green rushed over to help with me in the lead. It looked an horrendous crash and my heart was in my mouth. By the time I got to him, he was up and brushing himself down because he was covered in whitewash from the fence. His only concern was a typical riders reaction, 'why had we all rushed to him and not checked the bike!'

I suppose that during my speedway days I gave supporters a few scary moments but the boot was on the other foot that day. We sometimes laugh about it these days but I never instructed anyone else after that.'

Graham Miles, Canterbury and Hackney rider, was the tallest rider in speedway standing at six feet six inches. After the accident at Hackney in 1971 that ended Graham's career, Birmingham's Arthur Browning at six feet four inches took over the title in a sport where riders, like jockeys, are usually smaller than average.

Wisecrackers

Asked about the beginning of his speedway career Belle Vue ace Soren Sjosten said, *'In those days I was young and nice – nowadays I'm only nice.'*

Speedway

A mix-up over starting gate positions in the 2009 Speedway World Cup race-off in Leszno, Poland, saw English rider Tai Woffinden started heat 22 from the number two gate, when he should have been from number four. The race went ahead and the four laps were completed, only for complaints and arguments to the referee forced a rerun with the riders in their correct positions.

Danish team manager Jan Staechmann, who had tried to attract the referee's attention prior to the first running, said: *'The referee is the authority and it would be beneficial if he knows the rules.'*

Speedway

When being interviewed by a reporter about his shale career, Soren Sjosten said: *'Don't forget to mention my fishing. I'm mad keen on fishing, I go all the time.'* Asked about any cups and trophies that he had won from fishing, he laughed: *'Not that king of fishing – just poaching for salmon and trout!'*

Speedway

Well remembered track photographer Alf Weedon had a very distinctive green Mercedes with an equally distinctive number plate ALF ***** which Barry Bowles, like so many other fans, had seen many times around the tracks over the years.

City of London policeman Barry was driving his crime car one night in the late 1970s when, outside the Daily Mirror building he spotted that same green Mercedes pullover. He said: *'I happened to know there had been a big speedway event somewhere but probably not racing. I thought we would give him a fright so, as we were only yards away from him we put on the blue lights and two tones and screeched to a halt nose to nose with the Mercedes. My operator and I both jumped out, him to the passengers door and me to the drivers side. We were both shouting for them to get out of the car, and both bewildered occupants got out.*

Alf looked up into my face and there was a sudden look of recognition followed by a tirade of blankety-blanks and how he was going to get me back for that, followed by roars of laughter.

This little episode was brought up many time after but always in very good humour.'

Speedway

In the German league the law stated that riders must have a job outside of speedway, and Robert Mouncer, a former Boston team member, then captain of Diedenbergen, was happy to oblige.

He was found a job as a welder in a factory to comply with the law and he said: *'I have to be at work by 6.45 in the morning and that's a bit much – but leaving off at 4 pm is OK though.'*

Speedway

Pete Jarman, then with Eastbourne and riding at Ellesmere Port, had a painful dilemma. In his first ride of the night, from the number four gate, Pete started with the others but a lot of bunching at the first corner meant he was forced out, then, by the time he had regained control, he found himself the length of the back straight behind. He had almost caught up by the end of the race and was only about four lengths adrift when the tractor driver pulled out onto the track behind the leading three and right in Pete's path. His bike was all mangled up under the grader and Pete was trapped under the tractor wheels.

He recalled: *'I had to laugh when I saw the driver's face. He was in such a state that I didn't know whether to be angry or feel sorry for him.'*

Speedway

Geoff Bouchard had an innocent looking fall whilst riding for Swindon at Leicester in August 1999 – a fall that had unforeseen circumstances that almost cost him his life. Geoff slid off and went under the safety fence straight into a track lighting standard that was close to the outer edge of the track. In that *'innocent looking fall'* he punctured a lung, injured some bones in his back and broke four ribs.

Some time after, the doctor told him that his injuries had been a threat to his life and he said: *'It was a sobering thought. I nearly died, and you can do that only once!'*

Asked in 1967 about the ridiculous ban on Swedes in British speedway during 1965 - '66, Soren Sjosten cracked: ' I'm married now so these days I'm only half a foreigner.'

On the strength of his first maximum for his new club Diedenbergen, Robert Mouncer was given the captaincy of the team. *'It's nice being captain,'* cracked Robert, *'but you get all the best riders of the night in the last race, so if the result hangs on till then you have to get a move on or get the blame for not winning the match.'*

'I took loads of stick from speedway fans and some presenters when the word got out that I had done male modelling for some football catalogues!' confided Wales No.1 rider Philip Morris.

Kings Lynn and Boston rider Ray Bales, son of international shale shifter Billy Bales, when being compared to his father for both looks and riding style, cracked: *'There may be some similarities but don't forget that I'm five inches taller than him!'*

Old timer Arthur Atkinson recalled a tale of when he was riding in Australia during the winter of 1929. *'I arrived at the Sydney track and I couldn't help but notice that several of the local riders were grinning at me,'* he remembered. *'I went over to find out what was so funny and one of them asked if I was going to ride a certain type of machine. I told him that I was and what was wrong with that. I was told that the last two riders who had ridden that particular kind of bike were both in hospital. "Shall we phone for an ambulance now, just to save time?" he joked. But I had the last laugh. I went out and broke the track record. Also that trip I won the Australian Championship and the Western Australian Championship.'*

Ronnie Russell, boss man at Rye House was left with no referee so he drafted in his brother Terry to fill the vacancy to allow the meeting to go on.

Unfortunately Terry gave an almost dead heat decision to the wrong rider causing the rider to complain: *'What's wrong with you. Don't you like me?'* Wisecracker Terry replied: *'No, I don't like people with ginger hair!'*

Speedway

Barry Bowles who did some of his early referee training under the supervision of well-remembered referee Arthur Humphries, recalled that Arthur liked to get away promptly as soon as possible at the end of the last race. He said, *'There was a saying doing the rounds at the time which said - if riders could get out of the starting gate as swiftly as Arthur Humphries gets out of the stadium, they'd win every race!'*

HACKNEY SPEEDWAY
Telephone : 01-985 9822

Dear..

Please note that you are booked to ride as follows:

	date	time
Hackney Friday	29th April	8 pm Start

Please take this as our official confirmation that you are booked to ride in the above mentioned meetings as per S.C.B. regulations.

Signed ....

Riders Booking Form

Eric Boocock recalled how the weather could not always be relied on and often gave him cause for concern. *'When I was involved with training at Belle Vue, I would leave my home near the east coast and travel over the Pennines and down to the old Aces track in the Hyde Road fairground,'* he said. *I would leave home in bright sunshine and as I travelled west and getting higher, the weather would change to such a degree that I would sometimes be passing through driving snow and icy roads only to emerge eventually in bright sunshine again down the other side.'*

Watching the attempts of Les Ott (later to be renamed Red Ott by Johnnie Hoskins of Canterbury) to get a bike to slide at Hackney training school, George Barclay borrowed a cycle speedway bike and took Les to a grassy area alongside the Thames where he taught him to skid the bike without brakes, just as so many others had fun doing in early days. That was all very well but not appreciated by opponents and team mates when Les got a team place because he would chuck the bike over to enter the first turn, knocking off all those who had got there first. Skittles! Fortunately he went on to become a good rider, and a good gater, too.

On July 20, 2009 the Royal Navy were piped aboard the Lakeside Arena to help the Hammers repel the Pirates of Poole. Led by Commander Steve Pearson, ten RN personnel stormed the meeting carrying banners, flags and brand new body colours for the home team riders for the night.

Commander Pearson, himself a speedway fan from way back, and still likes to be on the terraces whenever his seagoing duties allow, said, *'We had a call from team manager John Cook and we were pleased to have the opportunity to put the brand out there, it generated lots of good publicity.'* The matelots put their banners on the air fence and a white ensign on the centre green flagpole.

Steve Pearson was invited to toss the coin for the last race nominations. He said: *'The night was a complete success from our point of view and the event tied in nicely with the first staging of Armed Forces Week.'*

Unfortunately, the good commander, a veteran of 26 years service and former warfare officer aboard HMS Ark Royal, couldn't rally his troops and arrest the Pirates in their tracks. The close fought meeting ended in a 45-45 draw.

Loyal Norwich rider Phil Clarke started with a few practice laps followed by a couple of second half rides in 1947 and by mid season he had progressed enough to earn a team place.

Ian Hoskins, son of 'The Father of Speedway' Johnnie, was probably speedway's first mascot when he was paraded at Wembley as a young lad. Later Ian became a promoter at various tracks, mostly in Scotland. He also promoted in Majorca and Rhodesia.

Bert Roger, middle of the three well known speedway brothers, received a back injury whilst riding at West Ham in August 1953 when the whiplash of his back tyre leaving the wheel knocked him off his bike. The blow was severe enough to force Bert to retire from the remainder of the meeting

Parkers Pension, a title that started out as a joke proved to be anything but a joke.

In 1946, when league racing got under way again after World War Two, a national Sunday newspaper, the Sunday Pictorial, introduced a Golden Helmet Match Race to be contested for on a monthly basis and carried a £6 per week prize to the holder. Jack Parker and Bill Kitchen were nominated to be the first contestants and Jack won the contest, then successfully repelled all attempts to remove that shiny new helmet from his grasp for the remainder of the season. In recognition of this feat Jack was given the Golden Helmet to keep and a new one was made.

Harringay's Vic Duggan managed to grab the shiny skidlid but relinquished the title soon after. Jack then beat his brother Norman for the vacant title. Another Australian Aub Lawson managed to unship Jack for a little while and then Split Waterman got in on the act, but apart from those annoying hiccups Jack Parker held the Golden Helmet Match Race title – and the £6 a week – almost continuously for a period of nearly five years .... hence the 'Parker Pension'

Unlike film stars, it's unusual to find speedway riders that have changed their name to a kind of 'stage name' but a couple that did – Bristol's Chris Boss and, a couple of decades later Plymouth's Kid Bodie – who started life as Walter Meads and Bob Coles respectively, had a very good reason for doing so .... they didn't want their mum to find out they were speedway riders. Not like Italian Guiseppe Marzotto who had a flirtation, if somewhat fleeting, with British shale in the 1970s. He used to ride under the *nom-de-plume* of Charlie Brown, presumably because no one could spell or pronounce his Italian version. Guiseppe had the last laugh because he went back to his native Italy and developed and produced the famous GM engine.

ack Parker is mostly remembered for his association with Belle Vue but what is not widely known is that .ck captained the first four teams that he rode for.

In 1929 when the first league was formed Jack became the captain of Coventry for three years before moving on to Southampton to skipper the Saints. A couple of years later saw ack as captain of Harringay then, in 1946 he was re-allocated to Belle Vue as the Aces skipper. Four teams and our captaincies in succession.

Swede Jan Andersson learned his craft at his local track Kaparna and rounded off his first racing season by winning the Swedish Junior Championship. The following year 1975, Andersson came to England with the Kaparna touring team and impressed enough for Swindon to offer him a berth. Unfortunately, at the season end the Swedish army made him an offer that *he couldn't refuse.*

The Swindon management pulled out all the stops to secure Andersson's early release from the military but at the last minute that release was over ruled and he was confined to a few meetings in Sweden, until his military duties came to an end.

When England raced against Sweden in a televised international match at Wembley on July 14, 1973, Peter Collins had to contest a run-off against Sweden's Anders Michanek after both teams finished the night with a 39-39 draw.

Collins made a very fast start and raced off with Michanek in hot pursuit until two laps later the Swede powered under the Englishman and sent him sprawling across the shale. Michanek was excluded for unfair riding and Peter Collins won the match for England whilst laying flat on his back.

Later in the season the pair had another two-man tussle when they had a repeat performance in the Knock Out Cup after both teams ended in deadlock, and again Peter saw off Michanek by just getting to the chequered flag first after an incredible amount of passes, totalling at least three or four times in every lap.

But the Swede Michanek got the last laugh because a year later he was crowned World Champion. Collins had to wait a further two years before world individual honours came his way.

Boxing Day 1956, Wimbledon staged an out of season meeting called 'The Christmas Vase', won by Bob Roger. Years later Bob, who meanwhile had suffered an almighty crash that finished his speedway career, was asked about that Boxing Day meeting. A surprised Bob asked: *'Why, what happened, did I win something?'*

1955 Norwich captain Phil Clarke had one appearance in the world final, held at Wembley. Around the same time he was elected chairman of the Speedway Riders Association – a position he held, like the captaincy of the Stars, until his retirement from the shale in 1959.

Of the SRA job he recalled: *'My role at that time was not so much as hard negotiator but more of trying to keep everybody happy. Lots of tracks were closing down and, naturally, putting riders out of work. I had to try and see both sides of everything, from both riders and promoters perspective.'*

Phil's spell in the SRA hot seat appeared to pass unremarkably but behind the scene his negotiating skills saved many an unpleasant incident, like walkouts or even strikes, from developing.

When Germany invaded his country during World War Two, Norwegian rider Basse Hveem dug a big hole and buried his speedway equipment so that the Germans wouldn't find it and have it confiscated. Years later at the war's end Basse dug everything up and found that his bikes had suffered no real damage.

Basse was also a force to be reckoned with on the ice until a serious crash cost him a kidney.

Ian Hoskins, who like his father Johnnie was always up for something new and different, pulled a masterstroke when he was promoting at Glasgow. For a double header Ian emptied the stadium after the first match and made everyone pay again before being allowed back in for the second match.

Aussie Jack Young is always credited with being the only rider to win the world championship whilst a second division rider and, of course, this is true. Jack is the only second division rider to win the coveted crown, which he did in 1951 as an Edinburgh rider.

But Jack was not the first second division rider to qualify and race in a world final. That accolade goes to fellow Australian Ken Le Breton. Glasgow (Ashfield) rider Ken competed in the 1949 final and with four third places and a last place in his second outing, came thirteenth with four points from his five rides.

New Zealander Geoff Mardon also gets in on the act as the only *third* division rider to *compete* in a world final. Geoff, an Aldershot rider, was second reserve in the 1951 final, held on September 20. He qualified for the final and was programmed as an official competitor – which means he competed in a world championship final although he never got to race.

2nd Test at Wembley, England v Australia 1955.

Eric Williams (Welsh), Tommy Price, Brian Crutcher,
Ken McKinlay (Scottish), Freddie Williams (Welsh)

Arthur Wright, Phil Clarke, Ron Mountford

(An England team that included two Welshmen and a Scot!)

Nigel Boocock is the holder of the Empire Speedway Medal.

Little Boy Blue was on yet another close season tour of Australia in 1978 when he was presented with the award at Sydney Showground for his contribution to Australian speedway over the years. That year Boocock was the English Lions tour manager but for many years he had been instrumental in taking riders to Aussie as a freelance touring squad.

Upon receiving the award Booey became a member of an exclusive club because only two other speedway riders had ever been honoured in that manner.

The two riders to precede him were Jack Parker and Ken McKinlay – making him the third member of a very exclusive club indeed.

Freddie Williams was second highest points scorer for Wembley from 1947 to 1956. During that period he amassed 1854 points from 237 matches. Freddie won the world championship twice – 1950 and 1953. He is the only Welshman ever to win the world title.

Ales Dryml, high flying Czech rider, couldn't speak any English when he first arrived on these shores with Leicester.

Nigel Boocock remembers a couple of occasions when he thought the *'Grim Reaper'* was riding passenger with him. He recalled the tale about when he thought he was dying, later to be immortalised in his 1975 testimonial brochure.

Nigel broke his collar bone at Wolverhampton on a Friday night and the following Thursday he had a World Championship semi-final meeting at Sheffield that he really needed to ride in, so he made up some sort of harness to help to support his shoulder, but on the night he came an almighty cropper and couldn't catch his breath. He says: *'I thought that I was dying because I couldn't breathe. Thoughts of that broken collar bone were foremost in my mind and I thought the broken bone had been banged through my lung and that was why I couldn't breathe.'*

Luckily he was only winded and a few minutes later he was up and ready to take his place in the re-run.

Later, in 1974, 'Little Boy Blue' was riding at Newport when he suffered yet another bone crunching fall. Not until he was back on his feet did his team mates come over. *'"We were afraid to come over to you because we thought you were dead," they told me after.'*

After World War Two the Wembley Lions operated for eleven seasons from 1946 to 1956. They were league champions seven times in their first eight seasons. 1948 was the year that they missed out and this was due to the Olympic Games being staged at Wembley Stadium, their home track. That year they undertook their home fixtures at Wimbledon.

Of the remaining three years they finished in second place twice and third place once.

Dick Wise, manager of Norwich and Yarmouth, writing in the 1948 handbook about Yarmouth's defeat by Poole in a home and away knock-out that April said: '(*that defeat*) ... *did not seem terribly important because of the great demonstration given by a young lad from Norwich – Billy Bales. Billy, only seventeen and a half years, is now a good team member well established in the hearts of all East Anglian speedway supporters.*'

Later, manager Wise said: '*... there is no doubt that Billy Bales has carried a few of the hard ridden matches won by Yarmouth.*'

A very nice birthday present for Cradley Heath's Erik Gundersen.

For his twentieth birthday, in October 1979, Erik received confirmation that he would not be required for military service with the Danish army after all. The Heathens management went to battle, on Erik's behalf, to argue his case for speedway over military and the Danish authorities capitulated.

Gundersen repaid the Cradley promotions kindness and the faith put in him when, five years later 1984, he won the world championship. He repeated the feat a year later 1985 and made it a treble in 1988.

Ten years after his third success at world honours, whilst riding for Denmark in the World team Cup Final, at Odsal Bradford, Erik Gundersen was involved in a three-man pile-up that almost cost him his life and put a premature end to his speedway career.

Premier League (2nd division) rider Darcy Ward stepped up in class and into the Elite League as a guest rider for Peterborough in August 2009. In his first ever ride at the East of England Showground and against top class opposition from the upper echelon of speedway, he showed everyone the way home; at the same time lowering the track record that had stood for almost two and a half years.

Ward, on loan from Kings Lynn, continued the meeting as he had started and finished the night with a very impressive paid sixteen points from six rides.

Not at all bad for his first time on that particular track.

Belle Vue rider and soon-to-be world champion Peter Collins won the Junior Championship of the British Isles in grand style at Canterbury on June 16, 1973. Peter dropped only one point – and that was to Canterbury track master Barney Kennett – and fifty quid, on his way to the Sunday Mirror Cup.

In a meeting that brought together the best under 21s from both divisions, Collins dropped his only point in an otherwise faultless night to Kennett in his penultimate race who, in turn fought hard for one point in his last race. Third placed rider, Kings Lynn's David Gagen had the misfortune to come up against the night's two high flyers Kennett and Collins in the same race.

Nigel Boocock recalled one of his finest moments in the early days of 1955 that he retold in his testimonial souvenir brochure twenty years later. He said: *'I made the second half final at Wimbledon and lined up against three of the superstars of the day, Barry Briggs, Ronnie Moore and Arthur Forrest, and who do you think was in the lead for nearly four laps? Yes me. Even when I fell off I couldn't be disappointed because I felt so great to have been out in front for so long. I don't think that I shall ever forget that race.'*

After a trip down-under in 1935, West Ham star Arthur Atkinson and a couple of his English team mates decided to return home the leisurely route via the South Sea Islands and then across America by car. Having done well in Australia they embarked on their journey with plenty of money.

Arthur later recalled in a magazine interview that they changed some Australian money for US dollars when they reached America but before they reached the east coast the dollars had almost run out.

They went into a bank and asked to change some Australian money for dollars but the bank had never seen Australian money before and refused; the same applied when an English five pound note was produced – they had never seen those before either.

The trio spent their remaining few dollars on petrol and a loaf of bread and had nothing else to eat for 24 hours. They drank water from streams.

Arthur said: *'What an experience. We were travelling through a civilised country with pockets stuffed with cash yet compelled to live on bread and water.'*

Cyril Roger, tough-riding – tough-talking, team member with Norwich Stars, crashed and suffered a broken jaw. A couple of weeks later he turned up to reclaim his team place and was reminded of his injuries. *'You don't ride a bike with your chin,'* he growled.

n an effort to improve what most people would call a successful riding style, Newcastle's Joey Owen enrolled in an Ivan Mauger training school.

Joey recalled: *'Ivan's aim was to make me stand up on the bike around the corners but I found that it was hard to alter my own style. I sort of mastered it in practice but it was a different story racing like that and I had a few crashes so I mixed the two styles and found myself on the way again. With my new style I top scored for Newcastle and won every individual meeting, at second division level, that I entered, including Wimbledon that I wanted so badly the previous year. I also retained the Silver Helmet that I had held all season and finished top of the second division averages – and to crown it all Newcastle won everything they wanted to win.'*

Brendan Shilletto tearaway trackman with Wimbledon and Canterbury in the late 1970s figured out a way around the *'no brakes on speedway bikes'* rule. *'All you have to do,'* he says, *'is stick your foot in the wheel!'* A trick he tried whilst riding for Wimbledon in the Gauntlet Gold Cup at Eastbourne – and it worked a treat.

After tangling with his team mate Stefan Salomonsson young Brendan shoved his foot through his back wheel. It stopped the bike dead but cost a smashed ankle, three broken toes and sundry other foot bones, plus a couple of months out of the saddle whilst the foot, and the wheel, got sorted.

Edinburgh's Tommy Miller went from absolute beginner to full team member and record breaker all in one season.

For the 1978 season Mildenhall riders had the added incentive of a kind of double bonus point payment. Local sponsors, the Palmer brothers, who donated 'The Palmer Trophy' each year, gave an extra bonus to home team riders for every point they scored above seven points.

At the season end Ray ales made himself a nice ttle nest egg by claiming the lions share with a ery impressive two hundred and fifty quid.

Hard riding Coventry reserve Ben Barker had a busy night at home against Poole and ended the meeting having taken seven rides, including a five rides from seven races spell, for a respectable eleven points tally. But his heat eight 'last corner cut back and dash to the line' to split the home pairing of Joe Screen and Steve Boxhall is what he will be remembered for.

A tired but ever-so-slightly modest Barker said: *'I made a race of it. I came here to ride. If there's a gap I'm going for it. There's a crowd here and a crowd at home on TV; they need entertaining – that's what I'm here for.'*

And that's what he did, at the same time earning himself a much deserved and well padded pay packet.

Reading ace speedster Dave Jessup had a nice Christmas present for 1978 – a brand new 350cc Bultaco. The trials bike, courtesy of Norman Flurry of Watling Tyre Services in nearby Gravesend, was put to immediate use over a pile of old tyres outside the depot before taking wee Dave to the winners rostrum in the Medway Motor Cycle Trial on Boxing Day.

In the Golden Jubilee World Final at Wembley Dave Jessup, the speediest of speedsters on that auspicious night, was denied a win in his first heat when his bike lost power. Later it was discovered that the cap on his push rod had cracked causing the disastrous engine failure.

Dave, who had high hopes of taking the world title in Golden Jubilee year said: *'Those caps only cost a couple of bob but that one cost me the world title and more than £100,000.'*

Jimmy Squibb's speedway career spanned a period from 1939 until 1975. Even allowing for the war years when he was in the army Jimmy still managed an incredible thirty years in the saddle.

A West Country man Jimmy spent the bulk of his racing life down in that neck of the woods, alternating between Southampton, Poole, Plymouth and Exeter. He did forays into other promotions occasionally, including a couple in London at New Cross and Harringay, and yet further afield to Ipswich and Cradley. In the process he totalled up more than 500 league meetings.

Jimmy ended his long career at Canterbury with his 'old pal' Johnnie Hoskins in 1974 and early 1975, where he paid his own expenses just to be able to ride. His last move was nearer to home with Weymouth but he didn't contest any league meeting in their colours.

Jimmy was still riding at 56 years old with thirty years continually racing and over 500 league meetings to look back on he established a record that is unlikely ever to be bettered.

Ron How, long time Wimbledon team member, lived on a farm but soon found that when he wasn't shifting shale he preferred shifting booze to shifting bales of hay. His family farm field backed right on to the garden of the local pub and Ron decided that pub life was a better bet than life on the farm, so he married the landlord's daughter.

Fifty years later and long after his track career had come to an end Ron still ran that same pub and only recently has he passed it over to his son. In return his son swapped houses and Ron – not forgetting the landlord's daughter – live just down the road and in the same village where he has spent nearly all his life.

Dave Jessup, cleaning a pile of old tyres at Watling Tyre Services, Gravesend

The tallest rider in speedway, six feet six inches Graham Miles, started his career with a few second halves at Canterbury in 1968. *'I won my first ever race,'* he said, *'then I asked to start on a twenty yard handicap mark next time and I won that as well.'*

Graham bought himself a second hand bike for a tenner and rode eleven matches for Canterbury that season. Soon after he entered his first grass international at Langon in the South of France where he broke the track record that was held at the time by Barry Briggs. That record (plus a couple of others) stood for many years.

Not one to let the grass grow under his feet – or water for that matter – Graham also turned his attention to ice racing. He went to Russia and qualified as reserve for the 1969 World Final. He scored seven points from his first meeting and five from the next one, and then travelled to Moscow for the final round where he sat comfortably with eight points from his first rides and with one more ride to come. He led his last race until his magneto let him down. Pretty good for a novice first-timer.

When Phil Collins signed for Cradley in 1978 he became the hottest – and most expensive – property in Speedway. His £15,000 plus fee instantly became a world record of the time. The eighteen year old had just become the third Collins brother to win the Junior Championship of the British Isles (later renamed the World Under 21 Championship and open to foreign riders), behind Peter (1973) and Les (1977).

The former Ellesmere Port rider lined up for his home debut with the Heathens on July 15 against Belle Vue, the team that has their own stars, brothers Peter and Les.

Tommy Price, Wembley high flyer and soon-to-be World Champion, had a love–hate relationship with Belle Vue riders and their track.

In 1945 Tommy, with Jack Parker as his partner, won the Best Pairs Speedway Derby at Belle Vue, and the following year, 1946, Tommy won the British riders Championship from Belle Vue riders Bill Kitchen (2nd) and Jack Parker (3rd).

In the late 1930s America really took the term 'dirt track' literally. One or two tracks had a covering of granite dust, but most, at that time, were genuine dirt tracks. The track surface was ripped up with the use of farm equipment – cultivators, harrows etc – so as to form a loose soil surface which was a couple of inches deep.

During the close season of 1976 and 1977 Phil Crump, riding in his native country of Australia at Broken Hill, New South Wales, broke the track record in the first of his four rides and then lowered it even further in each of his remaining rides. Then, for good measure, he entered a six lap race and whipped a staggering ten seconds off that record as well.

The Peterborough Panthers had a payday to remember when every rider was a winner or a paid winner, in every race. The most unusual scoreline of 40-0 came about because the visitors, Oxford, refused to race on what they considered an unsafe track in the National League meeting in September 1976. Having declared the track fit for racing the referee allowed the Panthers pairing to ride on their own to a 5-0 win in each race until the eighth heat when by which time the match was won.

The loyal fans that had come to support their team were given their entrance fee back.

Johnnie Hoskins, who was promoter at Belle Vue when Ron Mason was one of their ever present, had fond memories of those days: *'I liked Ron,'* he said, *'Ron was a useful middle order team member who always got his share of the points total. He had a good tactical mind and I think he would have made a good team manager.'*

Later, that accolade was put to Ron for his thoughts on the matter. *'Even if I say so myself, I was better as a coach than as a rider,'* he said, *'The good riders would put the bike where they wanted it, I had to go where the bike put me.'*

Ron was also a first class engine tuner and mechanic. His long time friend and team partner Jack Parker rode Ron's spare in one of his World Championship rounds because Ron's second bike was better than his own almost perfect machine.

The very first race ever staged at Poole when the Dorset track opened for business in 1948 ended in disaster when Yarmouth's Reg Craven was involved in a fatal crash.

Reg, brother of West Ham's Malcolm Craven, died on the first corner of the first lap of the first race.

Jamie Luckhurst, handy points grabber with Canterbury, had an unexpected windfall when toward the end of the 1984 season and having raced to a decent payday, young Jamie copped a second payout, this time from a secret admirer.

Dad, Reg Luckhurst, a former Wimbledon Don and by then team manager with the Crusaders said: *'It's happened twice now. He's received a couple of sizeable donations. Of course it's most welcome but we don't know who this admirer is. The only clue we have is the postmark on the envelope.'*

2007 was the seventh year that a round of the Grand Prix had been staged at the Millennium Stadium in Cardiff and every single race proved to be an absolute classic.

It was also the first year that Chris Harris had achieved a place in the line-up. Before the meeting he said that he was hoping for around ten points, or at least enough to qualify for the semi final. As luck, or skill, would have it he surpassed even his own expectations and finished the five heats with twelve points and more than enough to secure him that place in the semis.

In his first outing, in heat three, after a restart caused by a gate malfunction, Harris lead home two world champions, Jason Crump and Nicki Pedersen to start his onslaught off with a win.

Heat eight, his second outing, he went from last to second on the third bend and just failed to beat yet another world champion Greg Hancock to the tapes by half a bike length.

In his third outing from gate one in heat ten he made the gate first but lifted to allow Hans Andersen through, and then pushed Andersen all the way to the flag.

In a rerun heat 15 after Andreas Jonsson came off and was excluded, Harris was never far from Leigh Adams back wheel for yet another second place.

He made the gate both times, after a restart occasioned by movement at the start, in heat nineteen, his final heat, and made no mistake to lead from the tapes all the way home for his second win of the night and thereby securing his twelve points for the second semi-final.

In his semi from gate two, Harris powered his way to a close second place which secured him a place in the final where, again from gate two, he powered away like a scalded cat, despite an unnerving restart, to take the chequered flag and his place at the pinnacle of the winners rostrum in what has gone down in speedway history as one of the best Grand Prix rounds ever seen.

Bristol Rovers Football Stadium received the attention of more than 100 police for their average everyday football match during the afternoon. At night, for an average everyday Bristol Bulldogs speedway match, they had the services of a grand total of one, and he had nothing to do but sit in the stand and enjoy the racing.

Arthur Atkinson rode in his first test match against Australia, at West Ham, in 1936 and continued to be selected for almost every test from then on.

Shale shifters Tommy Price and Olle Nygren were accomplished road racers – but what about the other way round.

Tarmac specialist Steve Parrish, these days a TV pundit, had a dabble as a mechanic in speedway pits, and Ron Haslam and John Newbold undertook a few laps around Sheffield at the invitation of The Shay boss Eric Bothroyd.

Alan Johns, Crayford shale shifting, top class frame maker and engine tuner really knew how to get the best publicity possible for his prototype Inter 100 junior speedway bike, he got Eric Gundersen to test ride it for him.

Eric obliged and gave it an airing at the Wembley Indoor Arena to help with the sales drive, and Johns couldn't have asked for a better ambassador because a week or two later Eric Gundersen became world champion.

Most riders suffer from the ubiquitous 'gremlins' at some stage during their career, but not many can claim to have had their winnings curtailed by an 'earwig' – but Robert Craven can.

Ellesmere Port rider Robert was leading in the Junior Final at the end of the 1978 season when he came to a sudden stop through loss of power. Upon a close inspection of his engine the pit mechanic found a dead earwig stuck in his fuel line.

Joey Owen started his shale career in 1973 with Barrow but only a year later Barrow shut up shop and he, with his brother Tom, was transferred to Newcastle. Joey said he wasn't at all happy about that prospect because it entailed a trip of around 160 miles each way, just for 'home' meetings. However, he persevered and for his first outing in the Diamonds colours, he raced to a maximum, and before the season end he powered to eighteen more.

Although Joey had a few setbacks in his first year with Newcastle like: missing out on his rightful win in the Junior Championship of the British Isles due to a blow-out that deprived him of a cert fifteen points maximum, at Canterbury ; not quite achieving his plan of winning the Second Division Riders Championship that he had set his heart on at Wimbledon ; plus his team not winning the league title and getting knocked out of the KO Cup at the semi-final stage, he was still optimistic and agreed to stay with Newcastle for another year.

'After all it wasn't all bad news,' he said. *'They had our Thomas and me and we were first and second in the averages. Not bad considering that we were No 7 and No 8 the year before!'*

Wimbledon teamster Trevor Hedge remembered an unusual crash that happened whilst he was engaged in riding for the Great Britain team in Poland in 1966. *'We had a coach to travel in with a trailer on the back containing all the team bikes,'* he said. *'On the journey Ken McKinlay happened to look out of the window and shouted that the trailer was missing. None of us took any notice because Ken was always making jokes.'*

After about another ten miles Barry Briggs eventually got up to take a look because McKinlay was going crazy and sure enough the trailer wasn't there. We got the driver to stop, and when we checked we found that the tow bar had broken away from the trailer. The coach turned round and we went back and found the trailer in a ditch that was surrounding a sugar beet field. The bikes were upside down with some of the frames bent and wheels buckled.

We were there for a long time while the tow bar was welded back. Meanwhile, Ivan Mauger and McKinlay got one of the bikes started and went to the nearest village to get some water so we could make some tea.

People passing in trucks and cars were amazed to see two men on a speedway bike on the road – with, of course, no brakes.'

Controversy raged at the 1982 World Final in Los Angeles when Englands Kenny Carter caused a sensation by holding up the meeting for twenty minutes after clashing with eventual winner American Bruce Penhall.

Both riders lined up for heat 14 needing a win when a collision sent Carter sprawling and was excluded from the rerun. Carter had his appeal, saying it was Penhall's fault, overruled and then stood in front of the starting gate preventing the rerun from getting under way.

Eventually Penhall won the re-started race and with it his second World Title in succession.

Carter threatened to sue the referee for preventing him from winning the title, although it was not certain that he would have won anyway. With a microphone, he invited the spectators to come down and watch the videotape of the incident, which he claimed exonerated him. He finished the night in fifth place.

Wheelspin

Comeback line of the 2009 season, if not the decade:

A young lady television reporter talking on camera to a visiting team captain, said: *'You really need to win this meeting tonight, how do you propose doing it?'*

'Win more races I guess,' was the serious reply to what, on reflection, was a rather stupid question.

Speedway

Matej Zagar, Slovenian team captain for the 2009 Speedway World Cup event two at Peterborough, declared: *'We can't afford any exclusions or silly mistakes if we want to get to the race-off.'* Then, he got himself excluded at the gate in one race and suffered a puncture in another. Just to rub salt into the wounds of bad luck, he was contesting the team Joker Card, for double points when he picked up the puncture.

Speedway

Before his move to a permanent slot with Crayford Kestrels, Norfolk based speedster Richard Davey was second halfing at Kings Lynn when, before the start of a particular race, he was making the customary practice start along the back straight. But what he didn't know was that just on the bend was an electrician up a stepladder changing a bulb in the trackside lighting. Richard made a splendid practice start and powered full belt into the bend, only to come an almighty cropper. He said: *'I was picking up my bike and feeling rather foolish, only to receive a burst of applause from the crowd – they thought I had only just noticed the man on the ladder and had laid down to avoid him. It's true that I had only just seen him but I would have fallen off anyway!'*

Speedway

A television reporter talking about the competition among the riders in a particular leg of the Grand Prix series, enlightened viewers with the revelation: *'There's a lot of people vying for those points at the moment.'* Then after a few moments reflection added, *'That's obvious of course.'*

How would we understand the sport without them?

Colin Goody, later to make his presence felt at Oxford and Poole and other tracks, started his career as a junior at Brafield 1954. The very next year he headed their scorecharts.

World championship Preview 1937 stated: '…. 1937 was thought likely to see an English winner.'

Jack Parker was with Frank Charles and George Newton as fancied holders. On the day the Americans took the first three places with English riders taking six of the next seven placings. The previous years winner, Van Praag, was the man to spoil England's six man consecutive block by finishing in sixth place.

What a time to learn you have no lead in your pencil!

A young fan at the 2006 Latvian Grand Prix in Daugvapils managed to work his way through to his hero Greg Hancock, only to find that he had a duff pen when it came to asking for the ever popular American's autograph. Hancock, the meeting winner and a nice guy among a sport of nice guys, gave the young kid his goggles instead.

Bristol's Tom Oakley, who was a superstitious man, was reluctant to pick up a glove that he had dropped prior to his race at West Ham in 1952, saying that it was unlucky to do so. So it was picked up for him and handed back – a couple of minutes later Tom was on his way to hospital and the mangled wreck of what was left of his bike was being cleared from the track. So much for superstitions!

When Jack Millen first arrived at Sunderland, pre season on a very cold clear day, Len Silver asked George Barclay to take Jack and Jim Wells to get some breakfast. They were advised to go to the café on the beach where they found just one young lady serving who asked what they would like. Jack startled them with his reply, which sounded like something in a foreign language, *'Rarfesh!'*

The waitress was as baffled as George and Jim were and even with several repeats none of them could make any sense of it. Then the smiling Jim Wells enlightened them – 'raw fish'.

The information didn't lessen the bewilderment as they now thought it was all a joke. But no, raw fish was what Jack wanted and that was what he ate with *the poms* watching in awe.

In the 2009 World Cup event two at Peterborough, Slovenian captain Matej Zagar was excluded from a race for holding up the start. He said: *'There was plenty of time before the race but with only three seconds to go, the start marshal wanted me to move over. You can't move a bike in three seconds, so I got excluded.'*

More than half a century earlier, in 1952, Bristol rider Eric Salmon was fined £2 for creeping at the tapes then, later at the same meeting, he was fined another couple of quid for not coming to the start line quick enough.

There ain't no justice.

English born Rob Mouncer, shale shifting captain of West Germany's Diedenbergen, was invited to race at Brookstedt and, as soon as he set off on the 500 mile journey, the clutch on his car refused to function forcing him to drive the whole distance on the autobahn without it.

Despite making it to the stadium safely his problems still plagued him and, he said: *'The track was two inches deep in winter slush, and if that was not enough, I kept breaking chains and ended the day with only three points.'*

Then typical of Sods Law, for his return trip back to Diedenbergen the car clutch worked perfectly!

Coventry shale shifter supreme, Nigel Boocock reckons he is a bit naïve. 'I didn't know what nitro was until it was banned,' he says.

George and Terry Barclay were immortalised in the Guinness Book of Records as the first father and son riders to ride in the same team at the same time.

Riding for Sunderland away at Boston, on Sunday March 25, 1973, both Barclays lined up in the same heat, and son Terry scored his first ever league point when dad George failed to finish the four laps.

The Barclay boys rode in almost all of Sunderland's fixtures that season, which brought them another record – that of the most joint appearances at that time.

Danish international Kenneth Bjere finally got to contest a Grand Prix final when he made it to the 2009 Latvian round at Daugavpils on August 1. The diminutive Dane raced to a second place behind former world champion Greg Hancock, and in front of GP stalwart Tomasz Gollop and Grand Prix leader Jason Crump.

Poole pairing of Hans Andersen and Joe Screen raced to an easy 5-0 in their home leg against Coventry when both the visitors failed to finish. Ricky Wells fell and pushed off the track, then Oliver Allen's engine gave up the ghost, leaving the home duo hardly able to believe their luck.

Paddy Mills, hard riding Norwich teamster in the sports re-emergence after World War Two, later moved to live in Leicester where he helped to put a short lived Brafield on the speedway map. He later turned his attentions to Long Eaton who managed to stay around considerably longer.

Before the start of the English round of the 2007 Grand Prix – which was held in Wales anyway – the TV anchorman enlightened us with the gem: *'It's an all star line-up here tonight.'* Then after a few moments reflection, added: *'But to be fair all GPs are.'*

Who was it that said there should be an award for stating the blindingly obvious?

Wales No. 1 rider Philip Morris says, *'I can honestly put my hand on my heart and say I was one of the very few riders who was not softening tyres. This was before you had to fit the tyres at the track.'*

Swede Tony Rickardsson was the last rider to win the World championship before the introduction of the Grand Prix system. He took the title in 1994. The next year, 1995, the Grands Prix came into being.

Bristol Bulldogs made speedway history when they were the first league team in the country to have two Czech riders in their team …. how times change.

Terry Barclay and John Robson were involved pre meeting in a *vultures race* at Sunderland to determine that night's number seven and Barclay lost out. However, when visitors Stoke came with a team short of riders he was loaned to the Potters to make up their team.

Sunderland's Jack Millen took Terry aside and said, *'You are not going to beat me Terry, but play your cards right and ^'ll look after you.'*

True to his word Jack did just that and ^erry finished the meeting on ten points.

Brothers Tom and Joey Owen lived on the family farm of about 200 acres, and to help to keep fit during the close season, they would carve out a makeshift track on their land to practice on. They said that when the land was required for ploughing they would simply move on to another field and start all over again. This must have stood them in good stead during their heydays of the 1970s when they carved up the opposi-tions tracks on a regular basis.

Wal Morton, Norwich rider of the late 1930s, was a tip-top fitness fanatic and, if he hadn't chosen speedway as a career, could easily excelled at almost any other sport.

Wal, a strict vegetarian, as was his wife, was an amateur boxer of note and at one time held the Amateur Middleweight Championship. He was also a swimmer of some stand-ing, as well as being an outdoors type indulging in yachting and camping.

He started his speedway career at Coventry before moving on to West Ham, and then to Wimbledon where Norwich captain Max Gosskreutz bought him and introduced him to The Firs.

Grosskreutz was known for build-ing his own frames and built one especially for Morton who, being a first class engine tuner, tuned and maintained his own engines.

It was not long before Wal Mor-ton was handed the captaincy of the Stars and later went on to captain England against the Dominions at Norwich.

In those early days Norwich could boast of crowd attendances of thir-teen thousand plus, and when they visited Wembley the gate was esti-mated at thirty-five thousand.

Trevor Hedge, Norfolk domiciled trackman with Norwich and lat-er Wimbledon, was the only British rider to qualify for the 1970 World Final in Poland.

That year the World Championship was held in Wroclaw and was the first time the final had been staged in an 'Iron Curtain' country.

Old 'Hurri-Ken' Ken McKinlay came from a family of thirteen but never felt it to be an unlucky omen because, as he pointed out, that with mum and dad there was fifteen of them.

Halifax body colour of an elephant and their name Dukes both originate from the Duke of Wellingtons regiment.

Sheffield promoter Neil Machin recalled an amusing incident way back when he was Rob Woffindens mechanic.

'We were with Stoke up at Berwick and Rob Grant was up to his usual tricks of knocking people off when, in this particular race he powered right up under Woffinden. Everybody knew what was going to happen and you could almost hear a sharp intake of breath, then, when they were all but touching, Grant knocked the power off for a second and they both finished the race on two wheels. Later back in the pits, Grant admitted he thought about knocking his opponent off but told him he had thought better of it because he would have had no one to talk to in the bar afterwards.'

Ever since 'the best track in the land' was closed down in 1964, efforts have never ceased to find another site for a new venue in the Norwich area. Many sites have been proposed over the intervening years by potential promoters and supporters club members alike, all to no avail as far as the council were concerned. Even an 18,000 petition in favour of the return of speedway fell upon stony ground.

In order to try to persuade councillors to give speedway a fair hearing – many of whom had never been to a speedway meeting - they were invited to Kings Lynn and Ipswich stadiums in 1975. A couple accepted the invitation but others preferred to record noise levels outside the respective venues.

The prospective promotion company also laid on their own noise tests at different sites around the city, with four local riders taking part.

Riders involved were Robert Mouncer, Andrew Bales, David Gagen and Alan Belham. A newspaper report at the time stated that the tests were carried out in 'atrocious conditions' and the supporters club paid tribute to all four riders for battling the elements and awarded each a gratuity.

Ken McKinlay

England can boast of six world champions.

Tommy Price, 1949

Peter Craven, 1955 and 1962

Peter Collins, 1976

Michael Lee, 1980

Gary Havelock, 1992, and

Mark Loram, 2000, our first world champion via the GP route.

Of course we could make that list even longer if we include Peter Craven's second win of 1962 and Freddie Williams two wins in 1961 and 1964. Although he had ridden in Internationals in England colours, Freddie was Welsh.

After the demise of Norwich Firs, the title *'best track in the land'* must have gone to Canterbury. Just like The Firs and almost every other track in the land, Canterbury had wonderful supporters and a first class track. One supporter in particular was a Mrs Moon who used to sit just in front of the referee's box in the Grandstand and give the referee lots of good natured verbal 'advice'.

Over the years Mrs Moon had got friendly with Mrs Bowles, referee Barry's wife and one night in the mid 1980s she asked if it was permitted for Barry Bowles to accept a gift for services to Canterbury. Mrs Bowles said that she would accept the award on behalf of her husband and, to avoid any accusations of bribery from the visiting fans, she would not give it over until they arrived home after the meeting. Barry said: *'My wife Val said that I would be thrilled with the gesture, and I was too. When I opened the package at home it turned out to be a huge sweet lolly, at least six inches across. It had an inscription in big red letters that read 'GET STUFFED'.*

I loved and treasured that award for several seasons until it deteriorated. What a lovely memory.'

German rider Egon Muller was reputed to be the highest paid rider in the world in 1978. He had three long track world titles to his credit, 1974, 1975 and 1978 but said that he earned more from singing than from bike racing. He said: *'I'm sometimes doing three live shows a day this wintertime. I can concentrate on racing during the summer months.'*

Then he added: *'The good thing about being a singer is the money – and a much smaller safety risk!'*

Back at the end of the 1969 season Nigel Boocock was reflecting in a newspaper article about the financial situation that riders find themselves in. An average rider can earn about £30 a week and a star a great deal more. *'Speedway is worth about £4,000 to me in this country, and I've also bought land in Australia with money I earned from two trips out there,'* he says.

A bike costs about £350 and loses around £150 a year in depreciation; boots cost £6 and the steel shoe another £3. He pays £30 for his leathers and around £30 for his helmet. *'I know it's rather a lot for a helmet but, to me, a helmet is very important,'* he says.

Nigel's wife Cynthia remembered the early days, *'Nigel used to earn about £15 a week, and we lived in a caravan when we were first married,'* she said. *'Then about six years later was the turning point and the sport started to pick up again. Now we have everything we want.'*

windon team captain Martin Ashby started the 1977 season in sensational style – he staged a one-man strike!

Ashby turned up to ride in the Itex Trophy at London's White City only to be told that he was using an illegal silencer and that it must be changed. He said: *'I was told that some of the White City riders had protested to the referee about my silencer and I was offered the use of a different one, but they can't be changed that quickly. Anyway, do some riders have that kind of authority that they can dictate what equipment a rider can use? What happens if I turn up next time with leathers they don't like, will they get me chucked out again?'*

Martin's one-man protest over the silencer issue, which was destined to drag on for many years, had the backing of the Speedway Riders Association.

Ironically a blood group tag brought in by the sports governing body to save lives may have been the very thing that could have cost Canterbury rider Graham Banks his life.

Introduced by the Auto Cycle Union as a safety measure to help speed up the treatment of injured riders, the tag worn as a necklace happened to catch in a following riders footrest as Banks fell during a grass track meeting, held at Romney Marsh. .

The rider, who received other injuries in the crash, was given emergency treatment trackside and taken to Ashford Hospital. He was transferred to the Intensive Care Unit at Canterbury where he died later the same day.

The 29 year old rider's brother Trevor was competing in the same race and took his place in the rerun line-up unaware of his brother's condition.

These days foreign riders coming to England must have a fair understanding of the English language but, many years prior to that ruling, George Barclay remembers the day when his understanding of a foreign language helped to save the day. 'At some time in the seventies and early eighties Les Ott and I somehow became couriers for Tee Mill Tours on coach trips to world finals in Sweden and Poland.' he said. 'Those who remember those trips will recall that, the German–Poland border was guarded with armed soldiers, who seemed quite forbidding.

On the return from our Polish hotel Les and his group had left quite some time before my coach, and I didn't expect to see him at any time before we were back in England. Imagine my surprise when, some hours later, we pulled up at the border to see Les running towards our coach so concerned that he had been delayed here by the guards without them being able to tell him why he and his group were being held. Five minutes later they were on their way after I had managed to translate and solve the confusion. It transpired that on the entry to the country Les had paid too much fee, so on the way back they wanted to reimburse him. I think I recall Les saying something like "blow that I just wanted to get on our way"'.

As for my part it seems my two years in Germany were not exactly wasted!'

Not even a bomb scare could put Ole Olsen off taking the 1975 world title.

In front of a 85,000 wildly cheering fans the Great Dane roared to an impeccable fifteen point maximum at Wembley – a track that he admitted was not one of his favourite raceways.

A bomb scare that came to nothing; a track that he was not comfortable with; and the continual close attention of Anders Michanek, the defending champion, could not deny Olsen his place at the top of the rostrum, the Sunday Mirror sponsored Trophy, a Gold Medal and the winners cheque for just over a thousand pounds.

When Dave Jessup moved into his new bungalow in the heart of Kent he found that the place already had a name – 'Riding Light'. It was nothing to do with Dave' lack of physical stature, the previous owner had been a sea captain. Dave said 'Seeing as I am quite small it suited me on my bike so I decided to leave the name where it was.'

American Wilbur Lamoreaux climbed the podium for runner-up spot in the world final at the Wembley Stadium in 1937 as a member of the history making winning trio of Americans. The following year, 1938, he mounted the rostrum once again, this time for the third place.

After a lay off of something like a dozen years, Wilbur was at it again in 1949 when the championship started up after a break for the war years. Now over forty years old he still held his own, but an engine failure in his fourth outing probably cost him his third rostrum place in succession.

On track Birmingham's John Hart was George Major's boss. John was team manager. Off track George Major was John Hart's boss. John worked in Georges garage and showroom.

Jack Parker always told anyone who would listen, 'There are only two corners that matter – the first and the last.'

A meeting at Bradford in the Odsal stadium brought a big surprise to both Terry Barclay and Bradford top man Alan Knapkin. In heat one Jack Millen broke the tapes and was excluded, resulting in Barclay being put in his place.

As he was going along the back straight Terry realised he could not shut the throttle, but relied on luck to carry him round the bend with the other three riders.

Flat out he went into the first bend in front, all the while expecting Knapkin to come past him. He knew that the Bradford number one was close because he could hear his engine right behind him. Every lap was the same, hanging on tight and waiting for the overtake which never came until, having won the race he looked back to see Alan was only just coming around the last bend.

The engine Terry could hear had been his own!

As an Edinburgh rider and later whilst with West Ham, Aussie Jack Young never seemed to let anything bother him ; probably the most laid back rider of all time, on and off the bike. He always appeared to be taking things easy and just doing enough – enough that is, to win the World Championship two years on the trot.

Crasher Gresham was his name,
Came to Bristol to seek his fame;
With his pockets stuffed with pot,
He thought that he could beat the lot.

He rode the tracks night and day,
God help anyone in his way;
His one thought was to win the race,
To hell with the rest who couldn't keep pace.

His reputation spread far and wide,
Even his team-mates tried to hide;
When asked to race along with him,
They'd turn away with a sickly grin.

He needs a partner, Teaspoon cried,
Come on, one of you, you must ride;
The riders talked in vain but it was deadlock,
All right said Teaspoon, I'll chose Boocock.

They all cheered Booey from the heart,
He'd be alright if he was smart;
I'll have that bugger Booey said, just you wait and see,
I'll hit him with my helmet if he dares to come near me.

He and Gresham made the bend,
Look out! Booey, he's no friend;
It'll be a five-one to us for sure,
But Gresham wants first place more.

GRESHAM'S LAMENT

By
Nigel
Boocock

The race is fast and all are tense,
As Gresham sends Booey into the fence;
Booey's excluded, says the ref,
The crowd go mad, he must be blind and deaf.

Booey's protests can't be heard,
As Palmer won't believe a word;
To help him make his point more clear,
Booey belts him round the ear.

Now slowly back to the pit,
His back is hurt, his leathers split;
Sock him dad, came a heartfelt cry,
From little Darren, the light of his father's eye.

With his helmet in his hand,
And both feet firmly on the sand;
I'll finish him, don't worry son,
As Booey shouts to Gresham – 'Come'.

In just thirty seconds flat,
Gresham's laying flat on his back;
His teeth are out, he cannot laugh,
He'll not make the second half.

As soon as he was out of bed,
Back to the USA he fled;
Now Booey's cheered from East to West,
Everyone knows that he is the best.

Track Measurements

All tracks are different – just ask any rider and they will say the same.

Although to the casual observer there appears to be very little difference each track has its own quirky characteristics. Some have tight sharp corners while others have wide sweeping bends; some have a slight banking and others don't; some are restricted by being inside a greyhound track, while others are controlled by being outside of a football pitch; and various other complications which all contribute to the overall size and shape.

While all must conform to a width of twenty-five feet minimum the length varies considerably, as the table below shows. Bear in mind however, that some stadia have been bulldozed and a new one built nearby carrying on the same name, therefore care should be exercised. Of course, many of these tracks are no longer with us.

Wembley	378 yds	Middlesboro	335 yds
Plymouth	216 mtrs (was 413 yds)	New Cross	262 yds
Motherwell	430 yds	Lea Bridge	440 yds
St Austell	360 yds	Walthamstow	282 yds
Bristol	390 yds	Cardiff	400 yds
Berwick	440 yds	Exeter	396 mtrs (was 443 yds)
Kings Lynn	242 mtrs (was 335 mtrs)	Edinburgh	260 mtrs
Cradley	367 yds	Rye House	262 mtrs
Leicester	380 yds	Eastbourne	275 mtrs
Belle Vue	418 yds	Isle of Wight	385 mtrs
Belle Vue (H)	285 mtrs	Swindon	363 mtrs
Liverpool	466 yds	Poole	299 mtrs
Glasgow (A)	355 yds	Lakeside	252 mtrs
Southampton	333 yds	Scunthorpe	285 mtrs (was 440 yds)
Coventry	375 yds	Peterborough	336 mtrs
Coventry	301 mtrs	Berwick	368 mtrs
Bradford	370 yds	Crewe	430 yds (was 470 yds)
Wigan	394 yds	Castleford	240 yds
Boston	380 yds	California	364 yds
Wimbledon	305 yds	Yarmouth	327 yds (was 325 yds)
Norwich	425 yds	Stoke	312 mtrs (was 347 yds)
Canterbury	390 yds	Wolverhampton	264 mtrs
Rye House	284 yds	Somerset	300 mtrs
Crayford	265 yds	Workington	364 mtrs
West Ham	415 yds (was 440 yds)	Sheffield	361 mtrs (was 390 yds)
Sheffield	390 mtrs	Buxton	240 mtrs
Nottingham	380 yds	Redcar	273 mtrs
Newcastle	300 mtrs	Newport	285 mtrs
Hackney	345 yds	Birmingham	330 yds (was 350 yds) now 292 mtrs
Harringay	336 yds	Ipswich	305 mtrs (was 400 yds) now 285 mtrs

World Championships

All world finals were staged at Wembley from their inception in 1936 until 1960. Allowing for a ten year break 1939–1949 for World War Two, the Empire Stadium staged the World Championships continuously for the first eleven years that the competition was held.

1961 saw Wembley lose its grip on the meeting of the year when a move to Sweden was undertaken for the first time. Sweden was to stage the World Final seven times, 1961 at Malmo and the remainder, 1964, 1966, 1974, 1977, 1984 and 1991, all at the relatively new Gothenburg Stadium.

Poland got in on the act four times: three at Charzow in 1973, 1976 and 1986, with Wroclaw once in 1992.

Germany staged the event three times: once each at Norden, Munich and Pocking in 1983, 1984 and 1993.

England's Bradford collared their share of the spoils in 1985 and 1990 with Denmark's Vojens doing likewise in 1988 and 1994.

Los Angles and Amsterdam held the competition once each in 1982 and 1987 respectively.

Other than those 'old faithful' Wembley picked up the spots in between, 1962, 1963, 1965, 1967, and 1969. The Championship was back at Wembley again in 1972, 1975, 1978 and 1981 for the last time.

1961 saw the World Championship move out of Wembley for the first time and go to Malmo, Sweden, where for the first time since 1949 – when three Englishmen took the first three places in their home country – the Swedes romped home to the three winning places on their home track and in front of their home fans. Ove Fundin took the title with Bjorn Knutsson and Gote Nordin close behind.

The three Englishmen to set the benchmark were Tommy Price, Jack Parker and Louis Lawson, and to show the rest of the world they meant business, Englishman Norman Parker finished in fourth place.

To stretch coincidence even further, the same thing happened in 1988 when Denmark hosted the World Final for the first time. At the recently constructed track at Vojens the Danes also raced to the first three places in front of their home fans. In

World Final, Wembley, 1955
Ronnie Moore ~ Peter Craven (World Champion) ~ Barry Briggs

a closely fought contest Eric Gundersen powered to the championship rostrum with fellow Danes Hans Nielsen and Jan Pedersen in close attendance. The third and last time it was ever to happen anywhere.

It almost happened in 1982 when America hosted the world final for the first (and only) time. When reigning world champion Bruce Penhall won the meeting with fellow Americans Dennis Sigalos and Kelly Moran taking close order of third and fourth places. Unfortunately, England's Les Collins spoiled what would have been the American's history-making clean sweep by taking second place.

The Gothenburg Stadium on the southern tip of Sweden, is a purpose built stadium that caters for many different sports. The innovative design was by the winner of an architects competition, with the surrounding roof covering held up entirely from the outside; which

World Final, Wembley, 1958
Aub Lawson ~ Barry Briggs (World Champion)
~ Ove Fundin

107

World Champions

					GRAND PRIX	
1936	L Van Praag	1971	O Olsen			
1936	J Milne	1972	I Mauger		1995	H Nielsen
1938	B Wilkinson	1973	J Szczakiel		1996	B Hamill
1949	T Price	1974	A Michanek		1997	G Hancock
1950	F Williams	1975	O Olsen		1998	T Rickardsson
1951	J Young	1976	P Collins		1999	T Rickardsson
1952	J Young	1977	I Mauger		2000	M Loram
1953	F Williams	1978	O Olsen		2001	T Rickardsson
1954	R Moore	1979	I Mauger		2002	T Rickardsson
1955	P Craven	1980	M Lee		2003	N Pedersen
1956	O Fundin	1981	B Penhall		2004	J Crump
1957	B Briggs	1982	B Penhall		2005	T Rickardsson
1958	B Briggs	1983	E Muller		2006	J Crump
1959	R Moore	1984	E Gundersen		2007	N Pedersen
1960	O Fundin	1985	E Gundersen		2008	N Pedersen
1961	O Fundin	1986	H Nielsen		2009	J Crump
1962	P Craven	1987	H Nielsen			
1963	O Fundin	1988	E Gundersen			
1964	B Briggs	1989	H Nielsen			
1965	B Knutsson	1990	P Jonsson			
1966	B Briggs	1991	J Pedersen			
1967	O Fundin	1992	G Havelock			
1968	I Mauger	1993	S Ermolenko			
1969	I Mauger	1994	T Rickardsson			
1970	I Mauger					

means that there are no obstructions anywhere inside to spoil the view.

Speedway started life in the 'Twenties', then we had the golden era of the 'Fifties' soon to be followed by the equally super 'Seventies' and the 'Nineties'. Then someone coined the phrase 'Noughties' for the new millennium.

But three riders who were anything but naughty in the Noughties were Jason Crump, Nicki Pedersen and Tony Rickardsson. Those three riders sewed up the first decade of the new millennium between them. Current World Champion Jason Crump in 2009, 2006 and 2004; Nicki Pedersen in 2008, 2007 and 2003, and Tony Rickardsson, who started of with two wins on the trot in 2001 and 2002 before rounding up his treble in 2005.

As if to emphasise their dominance of the decade, in 2003 all three mounted the rostrum to take the accolades: 1st Pedersen, 2nd Crump, and 3rd Rickardsson.

METROPOLITAN POLICE
WEMBLEY POLICE STATION
603 HARROW ROAD
WEMBLEY, MIDDLESEX, HA0 2HH
Telephone 01-900 7212 (Switchboard)
        01-900   (Direct)

Your ref. :

Our ref. :
GN 73/1969/18

D.M. Lomas,

29th October 1975.

r Mr. Lomas,

In thanking you for your letter of 22nd October, may I say
t our records show that 81,313 people attended the World Speedway
mpionships at Wembley Stadium on 6th September 1975 and that 3,603 cars,
motor cycles and 215 coaches used the official car parks. There was
o considerable parking in streets nearby.

I was at the Championships and am happy to confirm that those who
ended were most agreeable and well-behaved, so that it will not be
prising for you to learn that there were no arrests nor evictions
m the Stadium. I only wish it were so for all events held there.

Traffic took some time longer than usual to disappear from
bley after the event, but this was due to the inordinately larger
bers of people who decided to use their own, rather than public,
nsport. I have not seen any complaints about the delay.

In hoping that my reply has been of some assistance,

I am,

Yours faithfully,

(R.P. Bryan)
Commander 'Q' Division

Confirmation of what
we all know - Speedway
Supporters are the best

Malcolm Simmons and Phil Crump Match Races at Canterbury